Plant-Based Cookbook

for Athletes

The Best Plant-Based Cookbook For Athletes To Improve
Heal, Increase Endurance and Strength With High-Protein
Recipes

By

Joshua King

Table of Contents

Introduction

Prioritizing a plant-based diet is not only a sustainable and more ethical choice for the environment, but it also provides the human body with a range of antioxidants, nutrients and fiber that can aid in healthy immune function, improve digestion, and enhance alertness and energy levels. Incorporating whole foods that are raw, unrefined, and unprocessed will provide the greatest benefit and absorption into the body without any immune side effects. Many animal products contain additives, stabilizers, preservatives and additional hormones that speed up the natural growth cycle of animal offspring in order to yield more meat product on the market. Not only are most animals treated inhumanely before slaughter, but they are also fed genetically modified grains and feed which are also absorbed into the human body when we consume these animals. The environmental impact of meat processing in factories and overpacked farm assemblies is also very detrimental, increasing greenhouse gas emissions, polluting the water with animal waste, releasing ammonia emissions, and clearing out natural rainforests and habitats endangering many species of plants and animals. Supporting organic and sustainable plant agriculture within our own local region has been on the rise for the last few decades and allows us to focus on the seasonal offerings of crop based on the climate of where we reside. Best of all, we can also plant seeds in our own backyard or balcony garden to reduce waste, overproduction, and eliminate our consumption of toxins and pesticides. It is also a creative and nurturing project to care for and harvest your own crop across the seasons.

Plant-based foods also include a higher amount of fiber that keeps the body feeling fuller for longer, in addition to vitamins and minerals, that many animal-based products lack in. There are many prebiotic fibers in plant-based foods such as artichokes, garlic, and onions that provide a healthy gut flora, allowing regular digestion, appetite regulation, and decreased blood sugar levels. They also help to fight inflammation which arises when the body breaks down tissues during your post-workout recovery. Green, leafy vegetables such as wheatgrass, spinach, kale, and chard can balance your blood pH levels, providing an alkalinizing effect and contain high amounts of calcium and magnesium as well. These minerals are important in enhancing bone health and density and creating greater relaxation in the body which provides better sleep at night. Plant-based foods also enhance your auto-immune system with antibodies in the long-term and provide more oxygen to the tissues, which help to fight free radicals and prevent the outgrowth of cancer and tumorous cells. Minerals such as iron, zinc, and selenium, found in high quantities in meat products are also apparent in plant-based foods such as whole grains, maple syrup, Brazil nuts, lentils, corn, garbanzo beans, bran flakes and green, leafy vegetables.

Other health benefits of consuming a plant-based diet include long-term weight loss and weight management. Overall, you will consume fewer calories but feel fuller for longer by eating foods high in fiber and protein. Plant-based proteins also take less energy and time to be broken down, allowing smoother digestion and metabolism into energy. While animal products, especially those that are heavily processed may contain trans fat which can lead to bad cholesterol, plant-based products will not create bad cholesterol unless you are overconsuming those with saturated fats such as coconut oil or corn oil.

Chapter 1.   What Is A Plant- Based Diet?

A plant-based diet is not synonymous to a vegetarian or vegan diet. Although these terms are often used interchangeably, they are not the same.

A plant-based diet is focused on proportionately eating more foods primarily from plants and cutting back on animal-derived foods. However, it does not necessarily involve eliminating entire food groups and lean sources of protein. This means, those on a plant-based diet may still opt to eat some meat.

Going vegan, on the other hand, means being strictly against animal products in any form—from never eating meat and dairy products to not patronizing products tested on animals and not wearing animal products such as leather.

A healthy plant-based diet generally emphasizes meeting your nutritional needs by eating more whole plant foods, while reducing the intake of animal products. Whole foods refer to natural, unrefined or minimally refined foods. Plant foods consist of those that do not have animal ingredients such as meat, eggs, honey, milk and other dairy products.

In contrast, those on a vegetarian diet may still eat processed and refined foods. Vegetarians can even eat fast foods, junk food and other salty snacks guilt-free.

Once you get started with this diet, you will notice a huge difference in how you feel each day. From the time that you wake up in the morning, you will feel that you have more energy, and that you do not get tired as easily as before. You will also have more mental focus and fewer mood-related problems.

As for digestion, a plant-based diet is also said to improve how the digestive system works. In fact, dieters confirm fewer incidences of stomach pains, bloating, indigestion and hyperacidity.

Then there's the weight loss benefit that we cannot forget about. Since a plant-based diet means eating fruits, vegetables, and whole grains that have fewer calories and are lower in fat, you will enjoy weight loss benefits that some other fad diets are not able to provide.

Aside from helping you lose weight; it maintains ideal weight longer because this diet is easier to sustain and does not require elimination of certain food groups.

Don't worry about not getting enough nutrients from your food intake. This diet provides all the necessary nutrients including proteins, vitamins, minerals, carbohydrates, fats, and antioxidants. And again, that's because it does not eliminate any food group but only encourages you to focus more on plant-based food products.

History of the Plant-based Diet

As you can imagine, humans have been consuming a plant-based diet before the invention of McDonald's and some of our other favorite fast-food chains. To begin our journey, I am going to start us off in the times of the hunter-gatherer. While we could go back even further (think Ancient Egypt!), I believe this is where a plant-based diet becomes most relevant.

Hunting and Gathering

The hunter-gatherer time period is where we find the earliest evidence of hunting. While we do have a long history of eating meat, this was a point in time where consuming meat was very limited. Of course, humans eating meat does not mean we were carnivores; in fact, the way we are built tells us differently. Yes, we can consume meat, but humans are considered omnivores. You can tell this from our jaw design, running speeds, alimentary tract, and the fact we don't have claws attached to our fingers. History also tells us we are omnivores by nature; however, the evolution of our human brains led us to become hunters so that we could survive.

The need for hunting did not come around until our ancestors left tropical regions. Other locations influenced the availability of plant-based foods. Instead of enduring winter with limited amounts of food, we had to adapt! Of course, out of hunger, animal-flesh becomes much more appealing. This early in time, our ancestors did not have a grocery store to just pop in and buy whatever they needed. Instead, they used the opportunity of hunting and gathering to keep themselves alive.

Agriculture

Eventually, we moved away from hunting and gathering and started to become farmers! While this timeline is a bit tricky and agricultural history began at different points in different parts of the world, all that matters is that at some point; animals started to become domesticated and dairy, eggs, and meat all became readily available. Once this started, humans no longer needed to hunt nor gather because the farmers provided everything we could desire!

Chapter 2. What Are The Benefits Of A Plant-Based Diet?

There are plenty of benefits associated with adopting a plant-based diet. Some people experience the positive effects of veganism earlier in the process, while others notice the advantages over a longer time frame. The benefits are common and unfold as your body becomes accustomed to the dietary changes.

• Weight loss is one of the major advantages of eating more vegetables and plant-based foods because they contain high amounts of fiber, which increases your metabolic function. Studies indicate that vegans have a lower body mass index and generally tend to be slimmer. This is largely due to the high level of fiber in vegetables and fruits, which make up a major part of the diet. Fiber helps your body process and absorb nutrients more quickly and efficiently than omnivorous or meat-based diets.

• A plant-based diet reduces your risk of cardiovascular disease. If heart conditions run in your family as an increased genetic risk, you can reduce the likelihood of a heart attack or artery damage by eating lots of fresh fruits and vegetables. Meats, and more specifically red meats such as pork and beef, contribute to the buildup of plaque in the arteries, which impacts the function of the heart. Over time, this narrows the arteries and reduces blood flow, which increases blood pressure and the risk of a heart attack.

• Vegan foods reduce inflammation caused by animal-based foods, which are highly acidic. Chronic conditions such as arthritis can cause the body to swell from inflammation, which can result in pain in specific areas of the body, and this can spread and worsen over time. While inflammation is the body's response to fighting infection and disease, it can occur incorrectly and over long time periods, thus causing constant pain. When it becomes chronic, pain management is often prescribed in the form of medication and modifications to the diet. Plant-based foods provide relief by reducing and even preventing or stopping inflammation completely once veganism becomes a regular part of your diet.

- There is a reduced risk of developing type 2 diabetes when switching from an animal-based or lacto-ovo vegetarian diet. In fact, some research indicates that the risk of developing diabetes is reduced by half. If you've already been diagnosed with diabetes, adopting a vegan diet is a much better option to manage your sugar levels. This is because the all-natural sources of sugar in fruits and vegetables are unprocessed and not excessive. When eating an animal-based diet, there is less attention to natural food sources in many cases, as vegetables and other foods take a second or third level of importance in many meals which place meat as the featured item. When you switch to plant-based eating, the quality of your food becomes more important because it's absorbed quickly, as the body digests it more efficiently than animal-based foods.

- Studies have shown a decreased risk of cancer in people who follow a plant-based diet and avoid animal and dairy products. This research indicates a link between eating red meat and cancer, due to the amount of trans fats and carcinogens these meats often contain. One of the most specific cancers that are prevented by eating a vegan diet is colon cancer. Carcinogens contribute to the accumulation of abnormal cell growth, forming cancer. In fact, proteins found in meat can increase the growth of cancerous cells and speed up the process, while vegan or vegetable-based proteins do not have the same effect.

- Eating vegan foods is better for digestion and promotes regularity while preventing constipation. This is also a great way to increase your metabolic rate and works well with a regular exercise routine. It's virtually impossible to become obese or significantly overweight while following a plant-based diet.

- You'll generally feel better and any bloating or gastric issues, including cramps, will usually disappear. A vegan diet is excellent for women of all ages and can alleviate the symptoms of menstrual cramps and discomfort as well as the side effects associated with entering menopause. A plant-based diet has all the ingredients needed to improve your way of life, including your mental, physical, and psychological well being.

Aside from the general benefits of a vegan diet, there are plenty of reasons why more athletes are going plant-based. It's become a much easier way to live and eat, with all the new meat and dairy alternatives and overall popularity. These reasons are research-based and the effects, when experienced, provide many advantages for an active lifestyle.

The benefits of a vegan diet are plentiful for bodybuilders, marathon participants, and all other types of athletes. Contrary to the myths and misconceptions about plant-based eating, there are many sources of protein, calcium, vitamins, and other nutrients to support the healthy development of muscle and tissue growth at a cellular level. A vegan diet is primarily based on natural, whole foods, leaving little or no room for processed products. It's also simpler to prepare and plan vegan meals while enjoying the advantages of creating new, delicious recipes and finding a wide range of options beyond dairy and meat.

What are the specific benefits of ditching animal products for plant-based eating? First and foremost, if you live and thrive in a physically active lifestyle, you'll need to increase your caloric intake. As an athlete, your BMI or bodyweight will be within a healthy range, and cutting calories is not recommended. At the same time, it's important not to consume an excessive number of calories, which is where a vegan diet provides some essential balance. By sticking with plant-based foods, you'll get all the nutrients and get the right amount of calories you need to maintain and improve your body and athletic performance.

An athletic lifestyle is a healthy way to live, though your risk of heart disease can remain the same if you continue eating an animal-based diet. In fact, bodybuilding and other strength training exercises can increase your heart's size and require it to function more and harder, which can be dangerous, especially if you eat a high amount of red meat and trans fats found in processed foods. A plant-based diet reduces this risk by close to 40 percent, which is significant and can help you avoid the potential for cardiac arrest in the future. You'll also have healthier arteries, blood flow, and nutrient absorption, which is due to your blood becoming more viscous or thick. When this occurs, your blood is able to transport nutrients more effectively throughout the body. This also keeps your cholesterol levels in check by preventing them from getting too high, which can contribute to many other health issues. As nutrients are better transported within the body, you will have a greater supply of oxygen which feeds the muscles and improves performance.

With a diet high in fresh fruits and vegetables, people who eat vegan will consume more antioxidants than their meat-based diet counterparts. For this reason, they are better equipped to fight and prevent diseases caused by the production of free radicals in the body. Free radicals are produced when processed, toxic foods are consumed. They can harm and interfere with the body's natural functions by encouraging the growth of tumors, cancerous cells, and various infections. Antioxidants, on the other hand, fight against and prevent the development of free radicals, protecting the body from them. When you increase the amount of these nutrients in your diet, you'll enjoy a greatly reduced risk of developing these conditions. Berries, citrus fruits, dark leafy greens, and pomegranates are great sources of antioxidants. Chia seeds are another excellent source and can be added to smoothies and plant-based desserts easily.

As you become familiar with all the options within a plant-based diet, along with these and other benefits, you'll find there are many useful options for vegan foods, including unlimited recipes and ideas, all of which are delicious and easy to prepare.

How to Prepare Before You Start a Vegan Diet

Before you dive into the world of plant-based eating, here are some important steps and suggestions to keep you focused and successful once you begin:

It's important to adapt to a plant-based diet on your own terms and at your own pace. Not everyone can ditch all animal products in one day and switch completely to vegan without making changes in stages over several weeks, even months. Every individual is different, and once you discover what works best for you, you'll be able to make those changes within your own time frame. For example, you may start by cutting down on meat or starting with dairy first. Cut out the animal foods that you don't eat as often, or eliminate one specific item at a time such as beef, chicken, or certain milk products.

Swap meat and dairy-based foods for a close vegan alternative. For example, if you normally enjoy a ham sandwich or tuna salad wrap, you may want to try hummus and smoked tempeh or tofu with sprouts as a tasty way to move into your vegan options. There are also vegan cheese slices that have similar flavors to their dairy counterparts, which can be used in the same way on subs, wraps, and sandwiches. A grilled portobello mushroom works well in place of a meat burger, and lentil stew instead of beef soup. Hummus and eggplant dips and spreads work as excellent replacements for mayonnaise and cheese options.

Don't be afraid to try new foods, including fruits and vegetables you may usually choose on your regular grocery trips. Shop at local food markets and stores specializing in imported goods. Try at least one new fruit or vegetable every two weeks, including something you might not usually eat. For some people, this might be eggplant, squash, or kale. Some of these options may not seem as favorable until you use them in a recipe. You'll discover a new exciting way to use plant-based foods. Squash, for example, may seem unappetizing to some because they haven't experienced the mellow aroma of butternut squash soup or as a roasted vegetable. If you don't feel initially comfortable trying a new food on your own, find a restaurant with the specific item in a dish. Buffets or vegan eateries are a good start and can offer many new ideas and flavors to try, inspiring and expanding your palate.

Get familiar with all the plant-based foods that provide essential nutrients, and make them a part of your regular shopping list. Beans, grains, greens, apples, berries, avocados, soy food, and other vegan options are a great foundation to build from. Consider your proteins, minerals (iron, copper, magnesium, etc.), vitamins, fiber, and other nutrients by organizing them into a chart or categories and listing foods that contain a significant source of each, as follows:

Protein - beans, soy (tofu, tempeh, miso),

Potassium - bananas, watermelon, potatoes

Vitamin C - oranges, lemon, lime, grapefruit, peppers, apples

Vitamin B/beta carotene - carrots, squash, yams/sweet potatoes

Antioxidants - berries, chia seeds

Healthy fats - avocado, flax seeds, hemp seeds, coconut oil, MCT oil

Iron - leafy greens, cabbage, beetroot

Do you have allergies or food sensitivities? Many people discover these early in life, and sometimes, intolerance for certain foods develop later in life. Peanuts, seafood, shellfish, and gluten items are common foods that certain people become allergic to or must avoid, either due to mild reactions or fatal consequences in some rare circumstances. Take note of any sensitivities you have and notice whether or not they are vegan. Many intolerances are dairy-related because some people experience difficulty with digesting lactose, which is a sugar contained in milk. Fortunately, you won't need to worry about animal-based foods that cause reactions. Going vegan most likely means reducing the number of foods you must avoid while allowing you to try new options.

Think about the plant-based foods you currently enjoy and make them a part of your diet right away. This includes meals you eat at restaurants, buffet options, and snacks you may enjoy on the go when you're commuting to work or school. Hot cereal, granola, bananas, hummus and crackers, guacamole, and vegetable side dishes are examples of what you may enjoy already and may continue to include in your diet when you completely switch to vegan foods.

Try adapting some of your favorite meat or dairy-based foods into vegan versions, such as a vegetable pasta sauce instead of meat sauce, or curried tofu instead of chicken. You may find referencing a recipe and substituting specific items with vegan options works best, or if you are a more experienced cook, try your own creations based on the dishes that inspire you.

Some people are comfortable with lacto ovo vegetarianism, which can be a step towards veganism. The lacto ovo method of eating includes dairy and eggs, without meat. For other people, a pescatarian diet works well by allowing them to eat fish while cutting out all other meats. Both of these forms of semi-vegetarianism are paths towards a fully plant-based diet.

Take time out of your schedule to explore vegan menu items, new vegan restaurants (these are usually more common than you'd think, especially in urban areas), and grocery items. While some vegan versions of cheese, dairy, and meat may seem unappealing at first, you may be pleasantly surprised by the variety of options that are available. The days of unappetizing, bland vegan substitutes are far gone, and a variety of flavorful, spicy, and aromatic blends of vegan cheese (soy or vegetable-based), coconut-cultured yogurts, nut-based and soy milk options awaits. Soy-based meat substitutes have greatly improved to the point of being indistinguishable from actual meat products, such as hamburgers and hot dogs.

Beans, legumes, and grains are an excellent and nutritious way to enhance your meals and build a foundation for them. Rice is one of the most versatile foods and can provide much-needed energy in the form of carbohydrates before a major tournament or marathon. Lentils, kidney beans, black beans, and chickpeas are all great sources of both protein and fiber. Use as many options as possible, including quinoa, couscous, oats, barley, and many other grains, as they will boost the nutrient and energy value of every meal. Explore veganism in your own way, and take your time so that you become familiar and comfortable with the switch from meat-based to plant-based. (Cook Creatively, 2016)

Ways to Boost the Benefits of a Vegan Diet

To maximize the benefits of a plant-based diet, there are some practices to keep in mind. These actions can increase the benefits of what vegan eating can do for your body and overall health:

• Eat raw whenever possible. Enjoying a meal with sauteed and stir-fried vegetables can be excellent, but if you can, try to increase the number of meals with raw food options, such as salads, hummus with a handful of peppers, cucumbers, carrots, and celery, or a fruit salad. Take advantage of raw produce toppings on veggie burgers or portobello mushroom patties. Enjoy an orange or apple in between meals as a snack or a pomegranate with your morning cereal.

• Add healthy fats to your diet. This includes monounsaturated and polyunsaturated fats, which help boost your cognitive function and provide many nutrients. You can find these in avocados, coconut oil, olive oil, nuts, and seeds. Incorporating a small handful of nuts and seeds or an avocado each day will ensure you get the right amount of fats you need in your diet. Flax and hemp seeds are also good options.

• To reduce sugar in your diet, use fruit as part of or all of a dessert option. For example, a raw, sliced mango with coconut cream is a tasty option, or try lightly baked apples sprinkled with cinnamon. A bowl of fresh berries in almond milk with or without cereal can be an excellent option for breakfast or a midday snack. If you're often on the go, bananas and apples are great options as well.

• Try a new food item once every week or two weeks. This might be something you've never tasted before, like a rare exotic fruit or vegetable, or a seed or nuts that are not commonly found in regular grocery stores. Make a point of visiting and shopping at foreign food markets and ask questions about trying new foods. Jackfruit, papaya, guava, and taro are examples of foods that are emerging in popularity in vegan cuisine and recipes.

- Add a handful of nuts and seeds to your diet whenever you need a quick snack. Making a habit of having a healthy source of eating available will make it easier.

Chapter 3.   Vegan Vs Plant-Based Diet

It is quite common for people to mistake a vegan diet for a plant-based diet or vice versa. Well, even though both diets share similarities, they are not exactly the same. So, let's break it down really quick.

Vegan

A vegan diet is one that contains no animal-based products (dairy, meat, eggs as well as animal-derived products such as honey.) Someone who describes themselves as a vegan carries over this perspective into their everyday life. What this means is that they do not use or promote the use of clothes, shoes, accessories, shampoo, and makeups that have been made using material that comes from animals. Examples here include wool, beeswax, leather, gelatin, silk, and lanolin. The motivation for people to lead a veganism lifestyle often stems from a desire to make a stand and fight against animal mistreatment and poor ethical treatment of animals as well as to promote animal rights.

Plant Based Diet

On the other hand, this type of diet shares a similarity with veganism in the sense that it also does not promote dietary consumption of animal-based products. This includes dairy, meat, and eggs. The idea here is to make a diet out of minimally processed to unprocessed fruits, veggies, whole grains, nuts, seeds, and legumes. So, there will be NO Oreo cookies for you. Whole-food plant-based diet followers are often driven by the health benefits it brings. It is a diet that has very little to do with restricting calories or counting macros but mostly to do with preventing and reversing illnesses.

Benefits of Vegan Diet

There are several benefits to a vegan diet, especially when it comes to nutrition. You will consume a lot of nutrients and far less saturated fats. As great as this sounds, it can be challenging for someone to give up their animal-based foods because they need to find alternative sources of their protein, vitamins, minerals, iron, and non-saturated fats. If they don't plan their new diet carefully, it could potentially cause them to face certain health risks.

The people who go on a vegan diet may do so for more than just health reasons. They may be taking a stand to promote environmental protection and stopping animal cruelty.

Nutritional benefits:

•Reduced saturated fats: vegan diet has less saturated fats which improve health, especially when it comes to coronary diseases

•More energy: more carbs in a plant-based diet provide energy to the body , fiber: high fiber vegan diet leads to healthier bowel movement and help in fighting against colon cancer

•Anti-oxidants: vegetables and fruits are rich in antioxidants that protect the body from some types of cancer

•Vitamins: vitamins boost the immune system, heals wounds faster and benefit skin, eyes, brain, and heart.

Disease prevention:

•Cardiovascular disease: improve cardiovascular health and prevent heart attack and stroke

•Cholesterol: eliminating animal foods means eliminating dietary cholesterol which improves heart health

•Blood pressure: vegan diet is rich in whole foods which is beneficial in lowering high blood pressure

•Cancer: switching to a vegan diet reversed many illnesses like reducing chances of prostate cancer, colon cancer, and breast cancer

•Arthritis: plant-based diet is very promising for improving health in individuals suffering from arthritis

Physical benefits

•Body mass index (bmi): diet without meats lowers bmi which is an indicator of healthy weight loss

•Weight loss: vegan diet eliminates unhealthy foods that tend to cause weight gain

•Healthy skin: vitamins and other essential nutrients from vegetables makes skin healthy, so vegans have good healthy skin

•Longer life: vegan lives three to six years longer than people who don't follow a vegan or vegetarian lifestyle

•Body odor: eliminating meat and dairy product from diet reduce body odor, and body smells better

•Hairs and nails: individuals who follow a vegan diet have strong hairs and healthier nails

•Migraines and allergies: vegan diet is a relief from migraines and reduces allergy symptoms, runny nose, and congestion.

Chapter 4. Plant-Based Nutrition For Sport

Carbs and Fats - What they Are and How they Impact Performance

For athletes to achieve energy balance, they also require the right number of proteins, carbohydrates, and fats. Macronutrients provide fuel for energy expenditure and athletes need to consume them in adequate quantities. If not, it limits the availability of energy.

Athletic Performance and Carbohydrates

Carbohydrates are an essential nutrient in an athlete's diet; they enable the body to perform to its optimal standard during physical activity for two reasons:

Energy: The brain and body require energy to function; when carbohydrates are consumed and digested, they are broken down into glucose, which is stored in the muscles and liver and used as fuel during physical activity. According to Michael Gleeson, Ph.D., and Jeukendrup, Ph.D., several studies indicate that fueling the body with carbohydrates for 45 minutes or more can improve athletic performance and endurance.

Muscle Gain: When there is a limited supply of glucose in the body, other nutrients such as muscle protein and fat are used as energy. When the muscles get the right amount of carbohydrates, protein can effectively perform its primary job of repairing and rebuilding muscle tissue, which boosts muscle gain.

Carbohydrates assist athletes in performing at their best by replenishing muscle glycogen stores, which is not possible on a low-carbohydrate, high-protein diet.

Fats: The Difference Between Good and Bad

During an athletic performance, the body's main source of energy comes from carbohydrates; however, when low-intensity workouts and extensive periods of athletic activity are performed, the main energy source is from fats.

Fat is an essential part of our diet; however, to enjoy the health benefits of fat, you must understand the difference between good and bad fats. Fats from meat and dairy products are called saturated fats, and they increase the amount of bad cholesterol (low-density lipoprotein, LDL) in the blood. Those who consume excessive amounts of saturated fats increase their risk of heart disease or stroke, states the American Heart Association. A vegan diet contains limited amounts of saturated fats; they are found in foods such as cocoa butter, palm oil, and coconuts. Therefore, it is advised that those on a plant-based diet refrain from eating plant-based foods high in saturated fats. If you are going to consume these foods, ensure that they make up under 30 percent of the fat you eat.

Many plant-based foods contain monounsaturated fats, which assist in lowering LDL cholesterol, which reduces the risk of stroke and heart disease. Foods containing monounsaturated fats include walnuts, Brazil nuts, and almonds, olive oil, avocados, and tahini.

Despite the negative effects of saturated fats, their main benefit is that they increase serotonin levels. Serotonin is an important hormone that plays a role in mood regulation and is known to alleviate depression, improve sleep, and reduce feelings of anxiety.

Finally, good fats enhance the bodies nutrient absorbing capabilities, with the main nutrients being vitamins A, D, and E; as fat-soluble vitamins, they are not absorbed by the body without the assistance of healthy fats. Vitamins A, D, and E are responsible for maintaining healthy skin, creating hormones, and boosting the immune system.

How to Consume Healthy Fats on a Vegan Diet

There are many ways you can consume healthy fats on a vegan diet; here are some of them:

Cook mushrooms, winter squash, and carrots in olive oil.

Eat nuts high in unsaturated fats such as almonds after a workout. Unsaturated fats are capable of reducing inflammation; therefore, you are likely to experience reduced muscle soreness.

Use flaxseeds instead of flaxseed oil, they are both rich in healthy fats, but flaxseeds are also high in fiber.

Increase your polyunsaturated fat intake to reduce high cholesterol levels.

Educate yourself about the foods that are rich in healthy fats.

The Potential of Proteins - Why they're Crucial for Athletes

The right nutrition is essential for athletes to perform at their best. They use excessive amounts of energy during long, intensive workouts; the body also experiences changes such as muscle damage. For the body to recover, it requires sufficient rest and nutrition, which enables the following:

Muscle restoration and growth

Limits the chance of illness and injury

Gets the body ready for another intense workout

For the body to recover, it needs to replace lost sweat with electrolytes and fluids, protein to rebuild and repair muscle tissue, and carbohydrates to replenish glycogen. When it comes to recovery, protein is vital because athletes require a lot more than the average healthy person who does a limited amount of exercise.

Protein: How Much?

Athletes should consume protein 30-60 minutes after a workout to get the maximum glycogen stores and to enhance muscle protein synthesis. Between 30-60 minutes after a workout is a perfect time to restore energy with protein and carbs because protein accelerates the process of muscles converting carbohydrates into stored energy. However, if you are unable to refuel during this timeframe, just make sure you get some protein in with your snacks and meals throughout the day. Here are the recommended amounts of protein you should consume:

1 gram per pound: This amount of protein provides you with enough to build muscle.

0.82 grams per pound: There is a lot of speculation about whether 0.82 grams is enough protein to facilitate muscle growth; however, research suggests that it is, but it's the lowest amount you should consume.

1.5 grams: If you consistently go overboard with your cheat meals, 1.5 grams per pound of protein will be of benefit to you.

The extra protein will probably not result in increased gains; however, increasing your protein intake will do the following:

Will keep you full for longer

Eating more protein will force you to eat less junk because your food choices are restricted

The thermic effect of food (TEF) suggests protein is not 4 kcal per gram but closer to 3.2 kcal per gram

If you are concerned about your protein intake, you can get all your daily requirements through a well-balanced, plant-based diet with sufficient calories. You will find plenty of delicious recipes in this book as well as a detailed nutrition guide.

Plant-Based Besties - The Protein Sources for Maximum Impact

Lentils - Cooked lentils contain the following nutritional values per 125 grams:

Fat: 0.5 grams
Carbohydrates: 20 grams
Dietary fiber: 8 grams
Protein 9 grams

The Health Benefits of Lentils

Lentils are rich in polyphenols that protect the body against radiation, ultraviolet rays, heart disease, and cancer. They also help with weight maintenance and digestive health.

Broccoli - Raw broccoli contains the following nutritional values per 90 grams:

Fat: 0.3 grams
Carbohydrates: 6 grams
Dietary fiber: 2.4 grams
Protein: 2.6 grams

The Health Benefits of Broccoli

Broccoli contains several powerful nutrients such as vitamin K, which is essential for the blood clotting process, and vitamin C – a powerful antioxidant that protects the body against harmful free radicals.

Nutritional Yeast - Raw nutritional yeast contains the following nutritional values per 15 grams:

Fat: 0.5 grams
Carbohydrates: 5 grams
Dietary fiber: 3 grams
Protein: 8 grams

The Health Benefits of Nutritional Yeast

Nutritional yeast is high in vitamin B12, which helps to regulate the central nervous system, boosts energy, digestive system maintenance, protects the body against breast cancer, colon cancer, and stomach cancer. Nutritional yeast is good for people with diabetes because it contains no sugar and is therefore considered a low glycemic food.

Peanut Butter Powder - Raw peanut butter powder contains the following nutritional values per 13 grams:

Fat: 1.5 grams

Carbohydrates: 5 grams

Dietary fiber: 1 gram

Protein: 6 grams

The Health Benefits of Peanut Butter Powder

Peanut butter powder contains fewer calories and fat than regular peanut butter, making it beneficial for those wanting to reduce their fat and calorie intake. Peanut butter powder provides the same health benefits as peanut butter. It contains several nutrients that help to boost heart health, such as vitamin E, magnesium, polyunsaturated fatty acids, and monounsaturated fatty acids. It is a good source of magnesium, potassium, and iron, which improves blood circulation.

Hemp Seeds - Raw hemp seeds contain the following nutritional values per 28 grams:

Fat: 12 grams

Carbohydrates: 3 grams

Dietary fiber: 3 grams

Protein: 10 grams

The Health Benefits of Hemp Seeds

Hemp seeds are a powerful source of essential fatty acids, such as alpha-linolenic acid, which is an omega-3. They contain no trans fats, and they are low in unsaturated fats. Hemp seeds contain a wide range of vitamins and minerals, such as vitamin E, potassium, magnesium, and folate. They are high in omega-3 fatty acids, which improve heart health and reduce inflammation.

Quinoa - Raw quinoa contains the following nutritional values per 219 grams:

Fat: 2.4 grams

Carbohydrates: 25.7 grams

Dietary fiber: 2.8 grams

Protein: 5.7 grams

The Health Benefits of Quinoa

Quinoa contains almost double the amount of fiber than the majority of other grains. Fiber helps to reduce high blood pressure and therefore lower the risk of a heart attack. Quinoa is high in iron, which helps maintain the health of our red blood cells. Iron also boosts brain function because it helps carry oxygen to the brain. Quinoa is known to alleviate migraines because it assists in relaxing blood vessels.

Sprouted Whole Grain Bread - Raw sprouted whole grain bread contains the following nutritional values per slice (34 g):

Fat: 0.5 grams

Carbohydrates: 15 grams

Dietary fiber: 3 grams

Protein: 4 grams

The Health Benefits of Whole Grain Bread

Whole grains are packed with nutrients such as antioxidants, B vitamins, magnesium, copper, zinc, and iron. Studies have indicated that a diet rich in whole grains helps to reduce the risk of cancer, obesity, type 2 diabetes, and heart disease.

Tofu - Raw tofu contains the following nutritional values per 85 grams:

Fat: 3.5 grams

Carbohydrates: 2 grams

Dietary fiber: 1 gram

Protein: 8 grams

The Health Benefits of Tofu

Tofu is an excellent source of amino acids, calcium, iron, protein, and other micronutrients. Tofu comes from soy protein, which helps lower bad cholesterol. It is low in calories and gluten-free. It also contains isoflavones that protect the body against osteoporosis, heart disease, and cancer.

Chia Seeds - Dried chia seeds contain the following nutritional values for 28 grams:

Fat: 8.4 grams

Carbohydrates: 13 grams

Dietary fiber: 11 grams

Protein: 6 grams

The Health Benefits of Chia Seeds

Chia seeds are high in protein. One of the many benefits of protein is that it helps to control appetite, and therefore, plays a role in the weight loss process. Chia seeds are also rich in omega-3 fatty acids; the combination of omega-3's and protein stabilize blood sugar and improves metabolic health.

Edamame Beans - Raw edamame beans contain the following nutritional values per half a cup (75 g):

Fat: 5 grams

Carbohydrates: 9 grams

Dietary fiber: 8 grams Protein: 12 grams

The Health Benefits of Edamame Beans

Edamame beans are high in protein and low in fat, and studies indicate that people who follow a high protein, low-fat diet achieve significant weight loss because they experience less hunger between meals.

Tempeh - Raw tempeh contains the following nutritional values per 84 grams:

Fat: 6 grams

Carbohydrates: 8 grams

Dietary fiber: 5 grams

Protein: 16 grams

The Health Benefits of Tempeh

Tempeh is a highly nutritious soy product that is high in protein, prebiotics, and a wide range of vitamins and minerals. Tempeh contains calcium, but it is dairy-free;

since tempeh comes from soybeans, it contains isoflavones, which is a natural plant compound that helps reduce cholesterol levels.

Chickpeas - Raw chickpeas contains the following nutritional values per 82 grams:

Fat: 2 grams
Carbohydrates: 22 grams
Dietary fiber: 6 grams
Protein: 7 grams

The Health Benefits of Chickpeas

Chickpeas are low in calories and high in protein, which accelerates the weight loss process. They are also high in fiber, and the combination of protein and fiber assist in weight management because they suppress the appetite. Chickpeas are also considered a low glycemic food which is beneficial for blood sugar management.

Peanuts - Raw peanuts contain the following nutritional values per 32 grams:

Fat: 16 grams
Carbohydrates: 6 grams
Dietary fiber: 2 grams
Protein: 7 grams

The Health Benefits of Peanuts

Peanuts are low in carbohydrates and rich in nutrients; they contain polyunsaturated fats and monounsaturated fats. They help to improve blood cholesterol levels, which reduce the risk of stroke and heart disease. Peanuts are full of fiber and protein and help with weight maintenance. The bonus is that they also make a satisfying snack.

Almonds - Raw almonds contain the following nutritional values per 95 grams:

Fat: 47 grams
Carbohydrates: 21 grams
Dietary fiber: 12 grams

Protein: 20 grams

The Health Benefits of Almonds

Almonds are very nutritious and high in vitamins, minerals, antioxidants, and healthy fats. Almonds are rich in vitamin E, a fat-soluble antioxidant that protects the cells from oxidative stress. Several studies have linked vitamin E with lower rates of Alzheimer's disease, cancer, and heart disease.

Spirulina - Raw spirulina contains the following nutritional values per 10 grams:

Fat: 0.8 grams

Carbohydrates: 2.5 grams

Dietary fiber: 0.4 grams

Protein: 6 grams

The Health Benefits of Spirulina

Spirulina contains powerful antioxidants that protect the body against inflammation, cancer, and oxidative damage. It has a positive impact on cholesterol by lowering triglycerides and bad cholesterol at the same time as raising good cholesterol. Spirulina assists in lowering blood pressure, which helps to reduce the risk of conditions such as stroke and heart disease.

Spelt - Raw spelt contains the following nutritional values per 100 grams:

Fat: 2.4 grams

Carbohydrates: 70 grams

Dietary fiber: 11 grams Protein: 15 grams

The Health Benefits of Spelt

Spelt is rich in many nutrients such as niacin, zinc, potassium, magnesium, and iron. It is known to help reduce the cholesterol absorbed into the bloodstream. Additionally, the high fiber content in spelt helps reduce blood pressure. They lower the risk of stroke and heart disease.

Potatoes - Raw potatoes contain the following nutritional values per 1 potato (148 grams):

Fat: 0 grams

Carbohydrates: 26 grams

Dietary fiber: 2 grams

Protein: 3 grams

The Health Benefits of Potatoes

Potatoes are high in compounds such as phenolic acids, carotenoids, and flavonoids. They play the same role as antioxidants and protect the body against free radicals, thereby reducing the risk of chronic conditions such as cancer, diabetes, and heart disease. The resistant starch in potatoes also helps to improve digestive health.

Kale - Raw kale contains the following nutritional values per cup:

Fat: 0.1 grams

Carbohydrates: 1.4 grams

Dietary fiber: 0.6 grams

Protein: 0.7 grams

The Health Benefits of Kale

Kale is one of the most nutritious plants in the world, and it contains 4.5 times more vitamin C than spinach. Vitamin C is an important water-soluble antioxidant required for essential cell functions. Kale is also one of the world's best sources of vitamin K, which is crucial for blood clotting.

Mushrooms - Raw mushrooms contain the following nutritional values per half a cup (48 grams):

Fat: 0 grams

Carbohydrates: 2 grams

Dietary fiber: 1 gram

Protein: 1 gram

The Health Benefits of Mushrooms

Mushrooms are an excellent source of folic acid. They are said to help boost the health of babies while in the womb. They are also high in selenium, and studies suggest they protect against cognitive decline, thyroid disease, heart disease, and cancer.

Seitan: Raw seitan contain the following nutritional values per 100 grams:

Fat: 1.9 grams
Carbohydrates: 14 grams
Dietary fiber: 0.6 grams
Protein: 75 grams

The Health Benefits of Seitan

Seitan is a good source of protein, and it is low in calories; it is one of the few meat substitutes that doesn't contain soy. Seitan is high in iron, which increases energy and enhances athletic performance.

Chapter 5. The Incredible Health Benefits

While starting a plant-based diet is an excellent idea and has many wonderful benefits let's be honest, you are mostly here to benefit yourself. It is fantastic that you are deciding to put you and your health first! You deserve to be the best version of yourself, with a little bit of legwork, you will be there in no time!

To some people, a plant-based diet is just another fad diet. There are so many diets on the market right now, why is plant-based any different? Whether you are looking to lose weight, reverse disease, or just love animals.

A plant-based diet is so much more than just eating fruits and vegetables. This is a lifestyle where you are encouraged to journey to a better version of yourself. As you improve your eating habits, you will need something to do with all of your new found energy! It is time to gain control over your eating habits and figure out how food truly does affect our daily lives! Below, you will find the amazing benefits a plant-based diet has to offer you.

Lower Your Cholesterol

Let me start by asking you a question; how much do you think one egg affects your cholesterol? One egg a day could increase your dietary cholesterol from 97 to 418 mg in a single day! There was a study done on seventeen lacto-vegetarian college students. During this study, the students were asked to consume 400kcal in test foods along with one large egg for three weeks. During this time, their dietary cholesterol raised to these numbers. To put it in perspective, 200 to 239 mg/dL is considered borderline high.

The next question you should be asking yourself is what is considered a healthy amount of cholesterol? The answer is zero percent! There is no tolerable intake of trans fats, saturated fats, nor cholesterol. All of these (found in animal products) raise LDL cholesterol. Luckily, a plant-based diet can bring your cholesterol levels down drastically. By doing this, you will be lowering your risk of disease that is typically related to high cholesterol levels. The good news here is that your body makes the cholesterol you need! There is no need to "get it" from other sources.

Healthy Antioxidants

As of recently, there has been a push with products showing they are incredibly healthy due to the fact they contain antioxidants. These are fantastic as antioxidants help prevent the circulation of oxidized fats that are building up in your bloodstream. As you consume more antioxidants naturally in your plant-based diet, this can help reduce inflammation, lower your blood pressure, prevent blood clots, and decrease any artery stiffness you may have.

To put it into perspective, a plant can contain about sixty-four times more antioxidants compared to animal products such as meat.

High Fiber Intake

As you begin a plant-based diet, you will be getting more fiber in your diet naturally. You may be surprised to learn that on average, about ninety percent of Americans do not receive the proper amount of fiber! This is bad news for a majority of people as fiber has some very good benefits. Fiber has been shown to reduce the risk of stroke, obesity, heart disease, diabetes, breast cancer, and the risk of colon cancer! On top of these benefits, fiber also helps control blood sugar levels and cholesterol levels.

Asthma Benefits

According to the Centers for Disease Control and Prevention, about ten percent of children in 2009 has asthma. This means that in 2009, more children than adults had the risk of having an asthma attack. Asthma is defined as an inflammatory disease. The question is, what is causing the rise of asthma? It's all in the diet!

According to one study, both eggs and sweetened beverages have been linked to asthma. On the other hand, fruits and vegetables both appear to have a positive effect on lowering asthma in children that eat at least two servings of vegetables a day. In fact, their risk of suffering from an allergic asthma attack was lowered by fifty percent!

Reduce Risk of Breast Cancer

While it can be hard to pinpoint the development of breast cancer, it seems there are three steps to creating a healthier lifestyle to lower your risk of developing it in the first place. First, you will want to maintain a normal body weight. Luckily, this can be achieved by consuming a plant-based diet. On top of eating your fruits and vegetables, you will also want to limit your alcohol consumption. By doing this, individuals have been able to reduce their risk of developing breast cancer by sixty percent! To put this into perspective, meat eaters have a seventy-four percent higher risk of developing breast cancer compared to those who eat more vegetables. I'm not sure about you, but that just doesn't seem worth it to me!

Reduce the Development of Kidney Stones

Did you know that by eating one extra can of tuna a day can increase your risk of forming a calcium stone in your urinary tract by a whopping two-hundred and fifty percent? The risk is calculated by studying the relative probability of forming a stone when high animal protein is ingested. The theory behind this is that urine needs to be more alkaline if you want to lower your risk of developing stones. When meat is consumed, this produced acid in the body. On the other hand, beans and vegetables both reduce the acid in the body, leading to a lower risk of developing kidney stones; science!

Reverse and Prevent High Blood Pressure and Heart Disease

Unfortunately, one in three Americans has high blood pressure. Studies have shown that as a diet becomes plant-based, this grants the ability to drop the rate of hypertension. In fact, there is about a seventy-five percent drop between an omnivore and a vegan! It appears as though a vegetarian diet sets a kind of protection against cardiometabolic risk factors, cardiovascular disease, as well as overall total mortality. When compared against a lacto-ovo-vegetarian diet, plant-based diets seem to also have protection against cardiovascular mortality, type-2 diabetes, hypertension, as well as obesity! This is fantastic news, especially when you lean that just three portions of whole-grain foods seem to significantly reduce the risk of cardiovascular disease in middle-aged people. This is the same benefit that a symptom-reducing drug can give you!

Control and Prevent Cancer

Fat from animals is often associated with the risk of developing pancreatic cancer. In fact, for every fifty grams of chicken consumed on a daily basis, your risk of developing pancreatic cancer increases by seventy-two percent! At this point in time, pancreatic cancer is the fourth most common death-causing cancer in the world. It's pretty simple to avoid if you simply switch your beef to beans!

On the other end of the spectrum, it appears that by consuming 70g of more beans a day can cut your risk of developing colon cancer by seventy-five percent. This may be due to IP which is found in cereal and beans. It appears this plays a major role in controlling tumor-growth, metastasis and preventing cancer. In addition to these benefits, IP overall seems to enhance the immune system, lower elevated serum cholesterol, prevent calcification and kidney stones, as well as reducing pathological platelet activity within the body. That seems pretty nifty for eating just a few more beans and less meat!

Decrease Insulin Resistance

Our bodies are very delicate machines. When fat begins to accumulate in your muscle cells, this interferes with insulin. When this build up happens, the insulin in the body is unable to bring the sugar out of the blood system that your body needs for energy. Unfortunately, high sugar intake makes this situation even worse and can clog your arteries altogether. When you eliminate meat from the diet, this means you will have less fat in your muscles. By decreasing these levels, you will be able to avoid insulin resistance in the first place!

Reverse and Prevent Diabetes

As of right now, diabetes is the cause of 750,000 deaths each year. Since 1990, the number of individuals in the United States diagnosed with diabetes has tripled to more than twenty million people. Within this range, you have one-hundred and thirty-two thousand children below the age of eighteen years old who suffer from diabetes. In 2014, fifty-two thousand people were diagnosed with end-age renal disease due to diabetes. Overall, the United States spent a total of two hundred and forty-five billion dollars in direct cost of diagnosing individuals with diabetes. If these numbers seem overwhelming to you, I have good news; plant-based diet can help with this issue. As you learn how to incorporate more vegetables into your diet, the risk of developing hypertension and diabetes drops by about seventy-eight percent.

Obesity Control and Weight Loss

In a study completed on various diet groups, it was shown that beans typically have a lower mass index compared to other individuals. These people were also proven to be less prone to obesity when they were compared to both vegetarians and non-vegetarians. This may be due to the fact that plant-based individuals have lower animal intake and higher fiber intake. When you reduce your caloric intake to lose weight at an unhealthy level, this has the ability to lead to unhealthy coping mechanisms such as bulimia and anorexia. As you learn how to follow a plant-based diet, you will be filling up on healthy foods such as vegetables, fruits, nuts, and whole grains. At no point on this diet should you be starving or wishing you could eat more. All of the food you will be consuming are typically low in fat and will help with weight loss.

Healthier Bones

One of the common misconceptions around a plant-based diet is that due to the fact you will no longer be drinking cow's milk, you will be lacking the calcium your bones need to grow strong. While we will be going over this further in depth later, all you need to know now is that it simply is not true. While on a plant-based diet, you will be receiving plenty of essential nutrients such as vitamin K, magnesium, and potassium; all of which improve bone health.

A plant-based diet helps maintain an acid-base ratio which is very important for bone health. While on an acidic diet, this aids in the loss of calcium during urination. As you learned earlier, the more meat you consume, the more acidic your body becomes. Luckily, fruits and vegetables are high in magnesium and potassium which provides alkalinity in your diet.

Along the same lines, green leafy vegetables are filled with vitamin K that you need for your bones. Studies have shown that with an adequate amount of vitamin K in your diet, this can help reduce the risk of hip fractures. Along with these studies, research has also shown that soy products that have isoflavones also have a positive effect on bone health in women that are postmenopausal. By having a proper amount of isoflavones, this helps improve bone mineral density, reduce bone resorption, and helps improve overall bone formation. Overall, less calcium loss leads to reducing your risk of osteoporosis, even when calcium intake is low!

Do it for the Animals

Whether or not you are switching to a plant-based diet for reasons other than health, it never hurts to be kind and compassionate toward other sentient beings. At the end of the day, sparing someone's life is going to be the right thing to do, especially when they never asked to be brought into this world in the first place.

Unfortunately, this is the whole reason behind the dairy and meat industry. In all honesty, there is nothing humane about taking lives or animal farming.

Of course, this goes beyond meat products. There are also major issues with the egg and dairy industry where dairy cows are forcefully impregnated and then have their calves taken away so we can steal their milk. These animals have feelings and emotions just like we do, what gives us the right to use them for their worth and then throw them away like garbage when we no longer have a use for them? Do the animals a favor and eat more plants, it will be better on your conscious.

Along with these same lines, you never know what is going to come with your animal products. There are a host of toxins, dioxins, hormones, antibiotics, and bacteria that can cause some serious health issues. In fact, there is a very high percentage of animal flesh that is contaminated with dangerous bacteria such as E. coli, listeria, and Campylobacter. These are all tough to find some time because these bacteria live in the flesh, feces, and intestinal tracts of the animals.

With the bacteria being tough to find and kill, this eventually can cause food poisoning. Each year, the USDA has reported that animal flesh causes about seventy percent of food poisoning per year. This means that there are about seventy-five million cases of food poisoning a year, five-thousands of which result in death.

Do it for the Environment

We were given this one planet to live on, and we should be doing everything in our power to help protect it. During these trying times, it seems that half of the population believes in climate change while the other half thinks of it as fake news. As a plant-eater, it is our duty to do our part in saving the environment. Unfortunately, the meat and farming industry is going to be a hard beast to take down. Depending on the source, it has been proven that the meat industry is behind anywhere from eighteen to fifty-one percent of man-made pollution. This puts the farm industry ahead of transportation when it comes down to the contribution of pollution to the greenhouse effect. In one pound of hamburger meat that you are consuming, this equals about seventy-five kg of CO_2 emission. Do you know what produces that much CO_2 emission? Three weeks from using your car! Do your part, eat more plants and save the planet.

Improve your Mood

When you are making an impact on saving the animals and saving the environment, it is no surprise that your mood will enhance! As you begin to cut back on animal products, you will be abstaining from the stress hormones those animals are producing while they are on their way to the slaughterhouse. This factor alone will have a major impact on your mood stability. By eating plants, this helps individuals lower their levels of fatigue, hostility, anger, depression, anxiety, and overall tension. The mood boost may be due to the antioxidants mentioned earlier in this chapter.

On top of these added benefits, it seems as though carbohydrate-rich foods like rye bread, steel cut oats, and brown rice all seem to have a positive effect on the serotonin levels in the brain. Serotonin is very important in controlling mood which is why a plant-based diet may help treat the symptoms that are often associated with depression and anxiety.

Skin and Digestion Improvements

You may be surprised to learn that skin and digestion are actually connected! If you suffer from acne-prone skin, dairy may be the culprit behind the issue! If you have bad acne, try a plant-based diet. As you eat more fruits and vegetables, you will be eliminating fatty foods such as oils and animal products that may be causing the acne in the first place. On top of this, fruits and vegetables are often rich in water and can provide you with high levels of minerals and vitamins. By consuming more fiber in your diet, this helps eliminate toxins in your body and boost digestion. When this happens, it could clear up your acne!

Improve Overall Fitness

Amazing things will happen as you lose weight and clean yourself from the inside out. When people first begin a plant-based diet, there is a common misconception that a lack of animal products means a lack of muscle mass and energy. Luckily, the opposite is true. It seems as though meat and dairy are both harder to digest. When these products are harder to digest, this means that it is taking more energy to do so. As you consume more fruits and vegetables on a plant-based diet, you will be amazed at how much added energy and strength you will develop.

On top of these benefits, a plant-based diet provides you with plenty of great quality proteins if you are looking to build muscle mass. While eating legumes, nuts, seeds, green vegetables, and whole grains, you will easily be consuming the forty to fifty grams of protein per day that is recommended. Of course, this number will vary but depending on your goals; you will easily be able to consume plenty of protein on a plant-based diet.

It's So Easy

When you first begin a plant-based diet, you should just expect your friends and family to doubt your life choices. You will be amazed to learn just how easy it is to live plant-based in the modern age. At the grocery store alone, there are incredible plant-based options for you and your family. There are plenty of plant-based milk options, ice creams, mock meats and more. Now, you are no longer forced to cook at home if you wish to live this lifestyle. With each passing day, becoming a plant-based person is become much easier compared to earlier times.

Chapter 6. Creating A Healthy Plant-Based Eating Habit

A common misconception among many people – even some of those in the health and fitness industry is that anyone who switches to a plant-based diet automatically becomes super healthy. There are tons of plant-based junk foods out there which can really derail your health goals if you are constantly consuming them. Committing to healthy foods is the only way that you can achieve health benefits. On the other hand, these plant-based snacks do play a role in keeping you motivated. They should be consumed in moderation, sparingly and in small bits.

Decide What a Plant-Based Diet Means for You Making a decision to structure how your plant-based diet is going to look is the first step, and it is going to help you transition from your current diet outlook. This is something that is really personal and varies from one person to the other. While some people decide that they will not tolerate any animal products at all, some make do with tiny bits of dairy or meat occasionally. It is really up to you to decide what and how you want your plant-based diet to look like. The most important thing is that whole plant-based foods have to make a great majority of your diet.

Understand What You Are Eating All right, now that you've gotten the decision part down, your next task is going to involve a lot of analysis on your part. What do we mean by this? Well, if this is your first time trying out the plant-based diet, you may be surprised by the number of foods, especially packaged foods, which contain animal products. You will find yourself nurturing the habit of reading labels while you are shopping.

Find Revamped Versions of Your Favorite Recipes I'm sure you have a number of favorite dishes that are not necessarily plant based. For most people, leaving all that behind is usually the hardest part. However, there is still a way you could meet halfway. Take some time to ponder what you like about those non-plant-based meals. Think along the lines of flavor, texture, versatility and so on; and look for swaps in the whole food plant-based diet that can fulfill what you will be missing.

Just to give you some insight into what I mean, here are a couple of examples: Crumbled or blended tofu would make for a decent filling in both sweet and savory dishes just like ricotta cheese would in lasagna. Lentils go particularly well with saucy dishes that are typically associated with meatloaf and Bolognese.

All in all, when this is executed right, you will not even miss your non-plant based favorite meals.

Build a Support Network

Building any new habit is tough, but it doesn't have to be. Find yourself some friends, or even relatives, who are willing to lead this lifestyle with you. This will help you stay focused and motivated while also providing emotional support and some form of accountability. You can do fun stuff like trying out and sharing new recipes with these friends or even hitting up restaurants that offer a variety of plant-based options. You can even go a step further and look up local plant-based groups on social media to help you expand your knowledge and support network.

Chapter 7. Plant-Based Meal Plan For Weight Loss

Vegan athletes need to be aware of what they eat and how much they eat to absorb the required nutrition that supports muscle function, repair, endurance, strength, and motivation as these are qualities that professional athletes treasure. Protein features high on the list of what to eat (Preiato, 2019). You should also consider your calorie macro and micro nutritional sources and amino acids, some of which may need to be supplemented. Proteins and carbohydrates average at four calories per gram, while fats average at nine calories per gram. Following this, it is possible to calculate how much of each nutrient type to consume per day.

When planning your vegan diet, an athlete may need to consider their exercise routines, as those who gym may have high impact days (such as the dreaded "leg-day") and lower impact days where their bodies need more nutrients geared at repair work. For every athlete, their meal plans will be uniquely based on their age, weight, level of activity, food availability (veggies and fruits tend to be seasonal), and personal taste. You certainly don't have to eat buckets of beans to be a vegan.

Pulling It All Together Into Your Meal Plan

In planning your vegan diet, you might consider the above graph, which guides your per daily grams for the average vegan based on a 1,525 calorie diet. For athletes, the amounts will increase to accommodate the calories burned during exercise. Hence, if you burn 500 calories running for an hour, you need to increase your diet by consuming an additional 125 grams of protein or carbs.

From the above graph, it is possible to plan meals based on the daily grams per nutrient type. You might get your base line 160 grams protein as follows: 1 cup wheat gluten (75 grams), 1 cup soy beans (68 grams), and ½ cup tofu (20 grams). The 100 grams carbs could be gained from: two slices of whole wheat bread (30 grams); one fruit, like apples, bananas, oranges, or pears (45 grams total); ½ cup granola (15 grams), and ½ English muffin (15 grams). Daily fat requirements can be made up by eating 100 grams of nuts and seeds (perhaps with the granola and fruit, yum!).

The 20 grams of amino acids could be spread throughout any of the plant foods consumed in this diet or supplemented via a nutritional supplement or dietary shake. These quantities would be split into three or more meals, depending on your metabolism and workout times. Increases to the calorie amounts depend on your activities. Simply rework the grams per day based on this. (Remember the fast rule: carbs and proteins (1 gram=4 calories) and fats (1 gram=9 calories). It is better to increase your carb and protein intake (in combination) than the fat intake.

Tips for Success

Converting to the vegan diet from an omnivore diet may, surprisingly, be a huge mental shock; however, there are some changes to your digestive system to consider as well. Vegans consume more dietary fiber than most omnivores, hence, your gut may go through stages of feeling somewhat bloated. You will need to consume more water as well. There are many suggested ratios, yet the easiest is to work per calorie. A fast rule of 1 milliliter water per calorie seems easy enough to follow. Keeping in mind that the volume of your food may increase, you may also need to eat quite a while earlier than an omnivore would before exercising. So, the usual rule of an hour fast before eating may need to be extended to 90 minutes fast before exercising.

Always consider adding variety to your vegan diet as this increases the opportunity for your body to consume all of the essential amino acids, and this leads to better protein synthesis (which is essential for developing muscle tone and recovering from injuries). Plant-based meals are very filling due to their high fiber content, yet you need to consume a larger amount to meet your calorie requirements. To avoid feeling too sated, you can gain extra carbs from eating nuts and seeds throughout the day as snacks.

Finally, when adding the finishing touches to your training program, it is essential that you intersperse training sessions with sufficient time to ensure that your muscles have time to rest and recover (where you rebuild their energy reserves, hydrate your body, and restore the normal chemical balance of your metabolism). Short-term rest periods may be anything from taking a few minutes break before moving on to the next training activity or even taking the rest of the day off after a particularly strenuous session. Professional athletes know that the body may be a machine, but it is a machine that needs to have "down time" too. It may be a good idea to keep a training log where you record what you have eaten, how long you fasted before training, and how you felt during and after the training session. This will also help you to evaluate whether you need to add more carbs or proteins to your diet, and if you require a longer rest period before moving on to the next training activity.

If you struggle with fatigue (or the shakes) after strenuous activities, you may need to increase your amino acid consumption or get more zinc and iron into your system. After all, we are all unique, and what works for another vegan athlete may not work for you. This training log can also allow you to experiment with perhaps moving to shorter training sessions with more frequent rest periods to achieve the same level of fitness and muscle building. No two professional athletes train the same way. Listen to your body and your gut to find a way that works for you.

Lastly, don't forget to get enough sleep. Mental fatigue can easily translate as physical symptoms. Insomnia may also be caused by a deficiency in magnesium. This could be caused by strenuous activity that consumes natural minerals in the body. Taking a magnesium supplement or eating some dark chocolate or half a banana before sleep can help create restful sleep.

Fortunately, the Internet allows for the development of support networks for vegan athletes. What we eat says a lot about us, and vegans can be successful, high-achieving athletes with planning and experimentation to find what works for their unique body.

Chapter 8. Breakfast To Motivate And Energize Your Body

Why is it Important?

There is a saying that describes breakfast as being the most important meal of the day. Why is that? After a good night's sleep, your body needs to be replenished with healthy levels to ensure the proper function of the muscles and brain. It is also partially dehydrated. The glycogen stored in the liver through carbohydrates is depleted. Cortisol levels are higher, as well. It is a hormone responsible for breaking down muscle.

According to Tim Ziegenfuss, "skipping breakfast drop kicks your coordination, stifles concentration, and puts a straitjacket on alertness." He is the International Society for Sports Nutrition's president. Then, skipping breakfast will weaken your muscle strength and endurance.

You see, breakfast is what gets your metabolism going. It is responsible for burning calories that you ingest throughout the day. On the downside, skipping breakfast will conserve calories instead. It is wrong to think that omitting breakfast means fewer calories because you risk having a higher body mass index. BMI is the ratio used to determine a person's healthy weight range. It is calculated by comparing their weight to their height. A higher BMI suggests you might be overweight. Those who eat breakfast are generally slimmer because starting the day with protein and fiber keeps your food intake in check for the rest of the day.

Other advantages to starting your day with a nutritious meal are a higher intake of calcium and fiber, the consumption of additional fruits and vegetables, and better performance in the execution of tasks. The same applies to exercise. It gives you energy, helps you stay focused and get things done. Eating breakfast also is linked to lower cholesterol levels and reduced risk of getting a chronic disease. Additionally, it facilitates mental faculties, such as concentration and memory.

However, those who don't have breakfast are more likely to make unhealthy food choices for the rest of the day. There is also an increased risk of developing other bad habits and risky behaviors.

Athletes realize that the best investment they can make is their health. That means fitness enthusiasts should favor a satisfying meal over a few extra minutes of shut-eye. Saying you don't have enough time to eat breakfast, aren't hungry, or don't like eating breakfast foods are excuses that will affect your performance.

Therefore, dieticians suggest you eat a more copious breakfast, one with anywhere between 500-700 calories. Not only will it provide you with energy, but limit cravings and keep hunger at bay. On the other hand, if you plan on working out first thing in the morning, a half-breakfast will suffice. Doing so will prolong your workout and enhance your physical activity. Even a simple breakfast is better than eating nothing at all.

Oatmeal

What are oats? They are considered one of the healthiest grains on the planet. They are sources of whole grains and are nutrient-dense. They also have a chockfull of vitamins and minerals, antioxidants, and fiber. Some health benefits that come with incorporating oats into your diet are a reduced risk of chronic disease, weight loss, and lower levels of sugar in the blood. Oats are good sources of fiber, protein, and carbohydrates. Antioxidants found in oats lower blood pressure.

They also contain soluble fibers that reduce cholesterol, increase satiety, and promote the growth of good bacteria in your gut.

A popular way of eating oats is in oatmeal. Here is a basic recipe for making oatmeal that you can customize to include the ingredients you love.

Casseroles

If you own a slow cooker, then you know how wonderful it is. Think of how practical it is for your food to cook overnight and be ready when you wake up the next day. Breakfast casseroles can be made ahead of time. Since it is cooked in one dish, you won't have as many dishes to wash. It is quick and easy to throw together and is bursting with flavor.

In some of our plant-based recipes like this one, you will see nutritional yeast on the ingredient list. What is it? It's from the same yeast used for brewing and baking, but with added nutrients. In this guide, we recommend vegans use fortified nutritional yeast as a source of vitamin B-12 that is typically only found in meat. Vegans are more at risk of having a deficiency of this vitamin in their diet. Nutritional yeast comes in different formats, such as powder, granules, or flakes. So why is it right for you? It is a complete protein because it has all nine essential amino acids. It also has minerals that help regulate the metabolism. In addition to this, this food has antioxidants, and it can strengthen one's immunity. It helps lower bad cholesterol, too.

In this recipe, it will be used as a cheese flavoring, without the dairy. Other ways that it can be a part of your everyday cooking is as a seasoning over popcorn, in giving an umami flavor in soups or as a thickener in sauces. Just one tablespoon or two of nutritional yeast will provide you with your recommended daily amount of vitamin B12.

Muffins

These aren't your typical coffee shop muffins that you grab with a coffee to go. No, these are much healthier! Our vegan breakfast muffins are kind on the planet, too — many baking recipes animal by-products, but not when you can substitute them with a vegan egg. Simply mix one tablespoon of flaxseed meal with 2 ½ tablespoons of water.

Bran cereal is a great breakfast choice for athletes. It is jam-packed with fiber and other nutrients like zinc and copper, selenium, and manganese. Its' flavor can vary between being sweet and nutty. In recipes, it is used to add texture and taste. Bran also aids in digestion, as it helps regulate bowel movement and reduces constipation. It is rich in prebiotics, which promotes a healthy gut. Eating bran on a regular basis can reduce your risk of getting certain types of cancer and can improve cardiovascular health.

Yogurt Parfaits

What is there not to love about yogurt? It is creamy and sweet. Vegans have found a way of enjoying yogurt without dairy products. This is thanks to nuts like cashews and almonds, amongst other things.

Why is vegan yogurt good for you? Some probiotics help keep your digestive tract healthy. The nuts used to make non-dairy milk such as almonds and cashews are full of protein, fiber, and healthy fats. They also contain calcium, antioxidants, iron, magnesium, zinc, and vitamins C and E. These nutrients are beneficial for regulating blood sugar levels, decrease the wrong kind of cholesterol and help burn fat more efficiently. Regular yogurt can have ingredients like artificial coloring and flavoring, which isn't right for you. It also has dairy, which we know is a food that is responsible for animal cruelty.

To make a yogurt parfait, you simply alternate between layers of yogurt with granola and fruit. It is a feast to the eyes as much as it is nutritious. You can buy non-dairy yogurt at the grocery store. Alternatively, you can make it yourself. There are many ways to go about it, but we'll keep this sweet and simple.

Pudding

Who says that pudding is only for dessert? With the right ingredients, this snack can be turned into a filling breakfast that will kickstart your day.

Let's take a minute to talk about chia seeds. This superfood is a significant element to include in a vegan athlete's diet. They have fatty acids from Omega 3, are a good source of antioxidants and are high in iron, fiber, calcium (18% of your daily intake) and protein. In just one tablespoon of chia seeds, you have 5 grams of fiber! Chia seeds can also be mixed with water to imitate the texture and moistness of an egg.

There are several ways of eating this versatile food. When raw, it can be used as a topping in smoothies, oatmeal cereal, and yogurt. In water, the seeds will expand and get a jelly-like texture. That is because chia seeds grow in volume. It is quite impressive when you think how this small seed can absorb up to 27 times its' weight from the liquid it is soaking in.

Scrambled Eggs

Eggs are a staple item in a person's breakfast routine and are known to provide athletes with protein and other nutrients. We will show you how vegans enjoy scrambled eggs by talking about tofu. This product comes from soya. To prepare the tofu, you need to press the soy milk into a block and then cool it.

The soy milk curd is what holds it together.

ofu varies in texture and firmness. Its' origins are from China but have been embraced by European and Western countries to promote healthy eating.

Tofu provides nine essential amino acids that the body needs to function correctly. It is also a good source of protein. Other nutrients that make tofu a popular food item in a vegan diet are its' other health benefits. It is rich in vitamin B1, copper, zinc, manganese, magnesium, and phosphorus.

Why do vegan athletes love avocados?

They have numerous health benefits, as well. Some of these include healthy fats and many vitamins. Avocadoes are good sources of Vitamin B-6, C, E, and K. They also have minerals like magnesium, potassium, riboflavin, and niacin. Plant-based foods such as fruits and vegetables are known to reduce the risk of developing chronic disease. Avocadoes do this and more. They also give you more energy, manage weight, and do wonders for your complexion. Monosaturated fats help satisfy hunger and stabilize blood sugar levels. Studies are even suggesting that avocados are beneficial for strengthening your immune system.

They are suitable for your cardiovascular health, too. The green fruit has beta-carotene, as well, which supports good vision. Vitamin K in avocados promotes bone health and can aid in preventing osteoporosis. A nutrient found in avocados, folate, helps decrease depression symptoms. It is high in fiber and can facilitate digestion.

Chapter 9. Food To Eat And Avoid

Why select in food options?

Any method that contains food and diet comes with a defined range of food options that you can select and avoid. It is necessary to pick up the right kind of food that will help you to get the desired results in the end. Making the food option is necessary as you have restrictions in the use of dietary options. Every meal plan defines the use of specific food options because all the food items have a significant effect on your body. Therefore, it is necessary to make the definition of the food options you need to use or lose in the meal plan.

Meeting nutrients

The basic need of selecting the food options is nutrition. When you are cutting off the other food options from the diet chart and moving towards the herbs and plants only then you need to choose the better options. Your body needs remain the same while the intake is different then you need to meet and match all the body requirements by selecting the nutrients that can help to get better with your overall body growth and its maintenance. The plant-based diet allows you to get all the necessary options that help you to meet the nutrient value your body needs.

Getting better taste

When you are taking a specific diet plan, it is hard to get the variant taste for your taste buds. It is important for you to make sure that you will choose the multiple food options that can help you to have better taste. The food selection you will make is to help you with a better approach towards the diet plan and it will not bore you.

Make new combinations

A plant-based diet helps you to get in shape, be healthy and improve your body's immunity as well. In contrast, it can make you feel sick, as you will be using only the plant products nothing else. In this regard, you need to have an idea about the best products. These multiple and best products will help you to make new combinations for your meals and help you to progress well with your diet option too. If you are not paying attention to new combinations, then it will not be possible for you to have continued interest in this diet plan. Soon you will get bored with the plan and want to quit and that can terminate your results. It is important to be consistent and maintain your interest in the food options you have around in order to get the best results.

Foods to Eat

If you are just getting started with the vegan diet, the food restrictions may come across daunting. Essentially, you will be limiting your food choices to plant-based foods. Luckily, there is a very long list of foods that you will be able to eat while following this diet. Below are some of the foods that you can include on your diet—so you go into your vegan journey, full of knowledge!

Vegetables and Fruits

Obviously, fruits and vegetables are going to be very high on your list. At this point in your life, you are most likely familiar with preparing some of your favorite dishes in a certain way. It should be noted that on the vegan diet, all dairy products such as buttermilk, cream, yoghurt, butter, cheese, and milk are going to be eliminated. With, there are some incredible alternatives such as coconut and soy. It will take a little bit of time to adjust, but you may find that you enjoy these alternatives even more—especially because they are going to be better for your health!

There will be many vegetables you can consume on the vegan diet. It will be important for you to learn how to balance your choices so you can consume all the nutrients you need. Within this chapter, you will be provided with a list of high-protein foods—but you will also need to consume foods such as kale, broccoli, and book choy to help with calcium levels.

Seeds, Nuts, and Legumes

As noted earlier, protein is going to be important once you remove animal products from your diet. The good news is that legumes are a wonderful plant-based and low-fat product for vegans to get their protein. You will be eating plenty of beans such as peanuts, pinto beans, split peas, black beans, lentils, and even chickpeas. There are unlimited ways to consume these foods in several different dishes.

You will also be eating plenty of seeds and nuts. Both foods help provide a proper amount of protein and healthy fats when consumed in moderation. It should be noted that nuts are typically high in calories, so if you are looking to lose weight while following the vegan lifestyle, you will have to limit your portions. These foods should also be consumed without salt or sweeteners for added health benefits.

Whole Grains

Another food that will be enjoyed while following a Vegan diet is whole grains! There are several products you will be able to enjoy such as wild rice, rye, quinoa, oats, millet, barley, bulgur, and brown rice! You can include these foods in any meal whether it be breakfast, lunch, or dinner! It should be noted that you will need to change how you serve some of your favorite foods. You will have to say goodbye to any animal-based products and instead, try to include more vegetables and olive oil. You can still have your morning oatmeal, but you'll have to make the switch to almond or soymilk.

Vegan Food Products and Substitutions

On the modern market, you will see several vegan-friendly products that have been manufactured. Some of these products include vegan mayo, whipped cream, "meat" patties, and other frozen foods. While these are great to have on hand, they are still processed foods. You will want to be careful of foods that have added sugar and salts. Any excessive additives will undo the incredible benefits the vegan diet has to offer. While, of course, they are always an option, you should try your best to stick with whole foods.

Foods to Avoid

Poultry, Meat, and Seafood

Obviously, this is a given. These foods include quail, duck, goose, turkey, chicken, wild meat, organ meat, horse, veal, pork, lamb, and beef. An easy rule you can follow is that if it has a face or a mother, leave it out. You will also have to leave out any type of fish or seafood. These include lobster, crab, mussels, calamari, scallops, squid, shrimp, anchovies, and any fish.

Dairy and Eggs

Removing dairy and eggs from a diet is typically one of the hardest parts of becoming a vegan. When you are unable to put your favorite creamer into your coffee, or simply make a batch of brownies because you must use eggs, you will notice the major difference. If you wish to become vegan, you will have to find alternatives for ice cream, cream, butter, cheese, yoghurt, milk, and any type of egg.

Animal-Based Ingredients

Animal-based ingredients are where you will have to be careful. I suggest learning how to read food labels so you can watch for tricky ingredients. You will want to avoid ingredients such as shellac, isinglass, carmine, cochineal, gelatine, egg white albumen, lactose, casein, and whey. You will also be avoiding animal-derived vitamin D3 as well as fish-derived omega-3 fatty acids.

Chapter 10. Breakfast Recipes

Amazing Almond & Banana Granola

Servings: 16

Calories: 248.9

Preparation Time: 5 minutes

Cooking Time: 70 minutes

Ingredients:

2 peeled and chopped ripe bananas

8 cups of rolled oats

1 teaspoon of salt

2 cups of freshly pitted and chopped dates

1 cup of slivered and toasted almonds

1 teaspoon of almond extract

Nutrition:

Fat: 9.4 g

Carbohydrate: 35.9 g

Protein: 7.6 g

Directions:

Preheat the oven to 275o F.

Line two 13 x 18-inch baking sheets with parchment paper.

In a medium saucepan, add 1 cup of water and the dates, and bring to a boil. On medium heat, cook them for about 10 minutes. The dates will be soft and pulpy. Keep on adding water to the saucepan so that the dates do not stick to the pan.

After removing the dates from the heat, allow them to cool before you blend them with salt, almond extract, and bananas.

You will have a smooth and creamy puree.

Add this mixture to the oats, and give it a thorough mix.

Divide the mixture into equal halves and spread over the baking sheets.

Bake for about 30-40 minutes, stirring every 10 minutes or so.

You will know that the granola is ready when it becomes crispy.

After removing the baking sheets from the oven, allow them to cool. Then, add the slivered almonds.

You can store your granola in an airtight container and enjoy it whenever you are hungry.

Perfect Polenta with a Dose of Cranberries & Pears

Servings: 4

Calories: 185

Preparation Time: 5 minutes

Cooking Time: 10 minutes

Ingredients:

2 pears freshly cored, peeled, and diced

1 batch of warm basic polenta

¼ cup of brown rice syrup

1 teaspoon of ground cinnamon

1 cup of dried or fresh cranberries

Nutrition:

Fat: 4.6 g Protein: 5 g Carbohydrate: 6.1 g

Directions:Warm the polenta in a medium-sized saucepan. Then, add the cranberries, pears, and cinnamon powder.Cook everything, stirring occasionally. You will know that the dish is ready when the pears are soft.The entire dish will be done within 10 minutes.Divide the polenta equally among 4 bowls. Add some pear compote as the last finishing touch.Now you can dig into this hassle-free breakfast bowl full of goodness.

Tempeh Bacon Smoked to Perfection

Servings: 10

Calories: 130

Preparation Time: 5 minutes

Cooking Time: 40 minutes

Ingredients:

3 tablespoons of maple syrup

8-ounce packages of tempeh

¼ cup of soy or tamari sauce

2 teaspoons of liquid smoke

Nutrition:

Carbohydrate: 17 g

Protein: 12 g

Fat: 1 g

Directions:

In a steamer basket, steam the block of tempeh.

Mix the tamari, maple syrup, and liquid smoke in a medium-sized bowl.

Once the tempeh cools down, slice into stripes and add to the prepared marinade. Remember: the longer the tempeh marinates, the better the flavor will be. If possible, refrigerate overnight. If not, marinate for at least half an hour.

In a sauté pan, cook the tempeh on medium-high heat with a bit of the marinade.

Once the strips get crispy on one side, turn them over so that both sides are evenly cooked.

You can add some more marinade to cook the tempeh, but they should be properly caramelized. It will take about 5 minutes for each side to cook.

Enjoy the crispy caramelized tempeh with your favorite dip.

Delicious Quiche made with Cauliflower & Chickpea

Servings: 2-4

Calories: 156.3

Preparation Time: 10 minutes

Cooking Time: 30 minutes

Ingredients:

½ teaspoon of salt

1 cup of grated cauliflower

1 cup of chickpea flour

½ teaspoon of baking powder

½ zucchini, thinly sliced into half moons

1 tablespoon of flax meal

1 cup of water

1 freshly chopped sprig of fresh rosemary

½ teaspoon of Italian seasoning

½ freshly sliced red onion

¼ teaspoon of baking powder

Nutrition:

Fat: 8.5 g

Carbohydrate: 8.1 g

Protein: 7.5 g

Directions:

In a bowl, combine all the dry ingredients.

Chop the onion and zucchini.

Grate the cauliflower so that it has a rice-like consistency, and add it to the dry ingredients. Now, add the water and mix well.

Add the zucchini, onion, and rosemary last. You will have a clumpy and thick mixture, but you should be able to spoon it into a tin.

You can use either a silicone or a metal cake tin with a removable bottom. Now put the mixture in the tin and press it down gently.

The top should be left messy to resemble a rough texture.

Bake at 350o F for about half an hour. You will know your quiche is ready when the top is golden.

You can serve the quiche warm or cold, as per your preference.

Tasty Oatmeal and Carrot Cake

Servings: 2

Calories: 210

Preparation Time: 10 minutes

Cooking Time: 10 minutes

Ingredients:

1 cup of water

½ teaspoon of cinnamon

1 cup of rolled oats

Salt

¼ cup of raisins

½ cup of shredded carrots

1 cup of non-dairy milk

¼ teaspoon of allspice

½ teaspoon of vanilla extract

Toppings:

¼ cup of chopped walnuts

2 tablespoons of maple syrup

2 tablespoons of shredded coconut

Nutrition:

Fat: 11.48 g

Carbohydrate: 10.37 g

Protein: 3.8 g

Directions:

Put a small pot on low heat and bring the non-dairy milk, oats, and water to a simmer.

Now, add the carrots, vanilla extract, raisins, salt, cinnamon and allspice. You need to simmer all of the ingredients, but do not forget to stir them. You will know that they are ready when the liquid is fully absorbed into all of the ingredients (in about 7-10 minutes).

Transfer the thickened dish to bowls. You can drizzle some maple syrup on top or top them with coconut or walnuts.

This nutritious bowl will allow you to kickstart your day.

Onion & Mushroom Tart with a Nice Brown Rice Crust

Servings: 6

Calories: 245.3

Preparation Time: 10 minutes

Cooking Time: 55 minutes

Ingredients:

1 ½ pounds of mushrooms: button, portabella, or shiitake

1 cup of short-grain brown rice

2 ¼ cups of water

½ teaspoon of ground black pepper

2 teaspoons of herbal spice blend

1 sweet large onion

7 ounces of extra-firm tofu

1 cup of plain non-dairy milk

2 teaspoons of onion powder

2 teaspoons of low-sodium soy or tamari sauce

1 teaspoon of molasses

¼ teaspoon of ground turmeric

¼ cup of white wine or cooking sherry

¼ cup of tapioca or arrowroot powder

Nutrition:

Fat: 16.4 g

Protein: 6.8 g

Carbohydrate: 18.3 g

Directions:

Cook the brown rice and put it aside for later use.

Slice the onions into thin strips and sauté them in water until they are soft. Then, add the molasses, and cook them for a few minutes.

Next, sauté the mushrooms in water with the herbal spice blend. Once the mushrooms are cooked and they are soft, add the white wine or sherry. Cook everything for a few more minutes.

In a blender, combine milk, tofu, arrowroot, turmeric, and onion powder till you have a smooth mixture

On a pie plate, create a layer of rice, spreading evenly to form a crust. The rice should be warm and not cold. It will be easy to work with warm rice. You can also use a pastry roller to get an even crust. With your fingers, gently press the sides.

Take half of the tofu mixture and the mushrooms and spoon them over the tart dish. Smooth the level with your spoon.

Now, top the layer with onions followed by the tofu mixture. You can smooth the surface again with your spoon.

Sprinkle some black pepper on top.

Bake the pie at 350o F for about 45 minutes. Toward the end, you can cover it loosely with tin foil. This will help the crust to remain moist.

Allow the pie crust to cool down, so that you can slice it. If you are in love with vegetarian dishes, there is no way that you will not love this pie.

If you have guests, they are sure to marvel at your amazing pie made of mushrooms with a fine brown rice crust.

Tasty Oatmeal Muffins

Servings: 12

Calories: 133

Preparation Time: 10 minutes

Cooking Time: 20 minutes

Ingredients:

½ cup of hot water

½ cup of raisins

¼ cup of ground flaxseed

2 cups of rolled oats

¼ teaspoon of sea salt

½ cup of walnuts

¼ teaspoon of baking soda

1 banana

2 tablespoons of cinnamon

¼ cup of maple syrup

Nutrition:

Fat: 2 g

Carbohydrates: 27 g

Protein: 3 g

Directions:

Whisk the flaxseed with water and allow the mixture to sit for about 5 minutes.

In a food processor, blend all the ingredients along with the flaxseed mix. Blend everything for 30 seconds, but do not create a smooth substance. To create rough-textured cookies, you need to have a semi-coarse batter.

Put the batter in cupcake liners and place them in a muffin tin. As this is an oil-free recipe, you will need cupcake liners. Bake everything for about 20 minutes at 350 degrees.

Enjoy the freshly-made cookies with a glass of warm milk.

Omelet with Chickpea Flour

Servings: 1

Calories: 150

Preparation Time: 10 minutes

Cooking Time: 20 minutes

Ingredients:

½ teaspoon of onion powder

¼ teaspoon of black pepper

1 cup of chickpea flour

½ teaspoon of garlic powder

½ teaspoon of baking soda

¼ teaspoon of white pepper

1/3 cup of nutritional yeast

3 finely chopped green onions

4 ounces of sautéed mushrooms

Nutrition:

Fat: 1.9 g

Carbohydrates: 24.4 g

Protein: 10.2 g

Directions:

In a small bowl, mix the onion powder, white pepper, chickpea flour, garlic powder, black and white pepper, baking soda, and nutritional yeast. Add 1 cup of water and create a smooth batter.

On medium heat, put a frying pan and add the batter just like the way you would cook pancakes. On the batter, sprinkle some green onion and mushrooms. Flip the omelet and cook evenly on both sides.

Once both sides are cooked, serve the omelet with spinach, tomatoes, hot sauce, and salsa. Enjoy a guilt-free meal.

A Toast to Remember

Servings: 4

Calories: 290

Preparation Time: 10 minutes

Cooking Time: 15 minutes

Ingredients:

1 can of black beans

Pinch of sea salt

2 pieces of whole-wheat toast

¼ teaspoon of chipotle spice

Pinch of black pepper

1 teaspoon of garlic powder

1 freshly juiced lime

1 freshly diced avocado

¼ cup of corn

3 tablespoons of finely diced onion

½ freshly diced tomato

Fresh cilantro

Nutrition:

Fat: 9 g

Carbohydrates: 44 g

Protein: 12 g

Directions:

Mix the chipotle spice with the beans, salt, garlic powder, and pepper. Stir in the lime juice. Boil all of these until you have a thick and starchy mix.

In a bowl, mix the corn, tomato, avocado, red onion, cilantro, and juice from the rest of the lime. Add some pepper and salt.

Toast the bread and first spread the black bean mixture followed by the avocado mix.

Take a bite of wholesome goodness!

Tasty Panini

Servings: 1

Calories: 850

Preparation Time: 5 minutes

Ingredients:

¼ cup of hot water

1 tablespoon of cinnamon

¼ cup of raisins

2 teaspoons of cacao powder

1 ripe banana

2 slices of whole-grain bread

¼ cup of natural peanut butter

Nutrition:

Fat: 34 g Carbohydrates: 112 g Protein: 27 g

Directions:In a bowl, mix the cinnamon, hot water, raisins, and cacao powder.

Spread the peanut butter on the bread.Cut the bananas and put them on the toast.Mix the raisin mixture in a blender and spread it on the sandwich.

Amazing Blueberry Smoothie

Servings: 2

Calories: 220

Preparation Time: 5 minutes

Ingredients:

½ avocado

1 cup of frozen blueberries

1 cup of raw spinach

Pinch of sea salt

1 cup of soy or unsweetened almond milk

1 frozen banana

Nutrition:

Fat: 9 g

Carbohydrates: 32 g

Protein: 5 g

Directions:

Blend everything in a powerful blender until you have a smooth, creamy shake.

Enjoy your healthy shake and start your morning on a fresh note!

Chapter 11. Lunch Recipes

Stuffed Sweet Potatoes

Preparation Time: 30 minutes

Cooking time: 1 hour 16 minutes

Servings: 3

Ingredients:

½ cup dry black beans

3 small or medium sweet potatoes

2 tbsp. olive oil

1 large red bell pepper, pitted, chopped

1 large green bell pepper, pitted, chopped

1 small sweet yellow onion, chopped

2 tbsp. garlic, minced or powdered

1 8-oz. package tempeh, diced into ¼" cubes

½ cup marinara sauce

½ cup of water

1 tbsp chilli powder

1 tsp. parsley

½ tsp. cayenne

Salt and pepper to taste

Directions:

Preheat the oven to 400°F.

Use a fork to poke several holes in the skins of the sweet potatoes.

Wrap the sweet potatoes tightly with aluminium foil and place them in the oven until soft and tender, or for approximately 45 minutes.

While sweet potatoes are cooking, heat the olive oil in a deep pan over medium-high heat. Add the onions, bell peppers, and garlic; cook until the onions are tender, for about 10 minutes.

Add the water, together with the cooked beans, marinara sauce, chilli powder, parsley, and cayenne. Bring the mixture to a boil and then lower the heat to medium or low. Simmer for about 15 minutes, until the liquid has thickened.

Add the diced tempeh cubes and heat until warmed, around 1 minute.

Blend in salt and pepper to taste.

When the potatoes are done baking, remove them from the oven. Cut a slit across the top of each one, but do not split the potatoes all the way in half.

Top each potato with a scoop of the beans, vegetables, and tempeh mixture. Place the filled potatoes back in the hot oven for about 5 minutes.Serve after cooling for a few minutes, or, store for another day!

Nutritional value per serving: Calories: 498, Carbs: 55.7 g, Fat: 17.1 g, Protein: 20.7 g.

Vegan Mac and Cheese

Preparation Time: 10 minutes

Cooking time: 30 minutes

Servings: 4

Ingredients

6 oz. cooked whole-grain macaroni elbows

1 ½ cups broccoli, cooked lightly

1 ½ tbsps. extra-virgin olive oil

1 chopped yellow onion,

1 medium potato, grated

2minced cloves garlic

½ tsp garlic powder

½ tsp onion powder

½ tsp mustard powder

½ tsp salt

¼ tsp red pepper flakes

½ cup raw cashews

1 cup of water

¼ cup nutritional yeast

2 tsp apple cider vinegar

Directions:

Soak the cashews in hot water for at least 4 hours

Place the cooked broccoli and pasta into a large bowl.

Pop a large saucepan over medium heat and add the oil.

Add the onion and sauté for 6 minutes until soft.

Add a pinch of salt, the potato, garlic, garlic powder, onion, onion powder, mustard powder and red pepper flakes. Stir well then leave to cook for another minute.

Add the cashews and water and stir. Simmer for 5-8 minutes until the potatoes have cooked.

Pour into a blender, add the nutritional yeast and vinegar and whizz until smooth.

Slowly add the water to the sauce reaches your desired consistency.

Pour over the pasta and broccoli, stir well then enjoy.

Nutritional value per serving: Calories: 506, Carbs: 58g, Fat: 21g, Protein: 18g

Satay Tempeh with Cauliflower Rice

Preparation Time: 60 minutes

Cooking time: 15 minutes

Servings: 4

Ingredients:

¼ cup water

4 tbsp. peanut butter

3 tbsp. low sodium soy sauce

2 tbsp. coconut sugar

1 garlic clove, minced

½-inch ginger, minced

2 tsp. rice vinegar

1 tsp. red pepper flakes

4 tbsp. olive oil

2 8-oz. packages tempeh, drained

2 cups cauliflower rice

1 cup purple cabbage, diced

1 tbsp. sesame oil

1 tsp. agave nectar

Directions:

In a large bowl, combine the sauce ingredients and then whisk until the mixture is smooth and any lumps have dissolved.

Cut the tempeh into ½-inch cubes and put them into the sauce, stirring to make sure the cubes get coated thoroughly.

Place the bowl in the refrigerator to marinate the tempeh for up to 3 hours.

Before the tempeh is done marinating, preheat the oven to 400°F.

Spread the tempeh out in one layer on a baking sheet lined with parchment paper or lightly greased with olive oil.

Bake the marinated cubes until browned and crisp—about 15 minutes.

Heat the cauliflower rice in a saucepan with 2 tablespoons of olive oil over medium heat until it is warm.

Rinse the large bowl with water, and then mix the cabbage, sesame oil, and agave together.

Serve a scoop of the cauliflower rice topped with the marinated cabbage and cooked tempeh on a plate and enjoy. Or, store for later.

Nutritional value per serving: Calories: 531, Carbs: 31.7 g, Fat: 33 g, Protein: 27.6 g.

Sweet Potato Quesadillas

Preparation Time: 30 minutes

Cooking time: 1 hour 9 minutes

Servings: 3

Ingredients:

1 cup dry black beans

½ cup dry rice of choice

1 large sweet potato, peeled and diced

½ cup of salsa

3-6 tortilla wraps

1 tbsp. olive oil

½ tsp. garlic powder

½ tsp. onion powder

½ tsp. paprika

Directions:

Preheat the oven to 350°F.

Line a baking pan with parchment paper.

Drizzle olive oil on the sweet potato cubes. Transfer the cubes to the baking pan.

Bake the potatoes in the oven until tender, for around 1 hour.

Allow about 5 minutes for the potatoes to cool and then add them to a large mixing bowl with the salsa and cooked rice. Use a fork to mash the ingredients together into a thoroughly combined mixture.

Heat a saucepan over medium-high heat and add the potato/rice mixture, cooked black beans, and spices to the pan.

Cook everything for about 5 minutes or until it is heated through.

Take another frying pan and put it over medium-low heat. Place a tortilla in the pan and fill half of it with a heaping scoop of the potato, bean, and rice mixture.

Fold the tortilla halfway to cover the filling and cook until both sides are browned—about 4 minutes per side.

Serve the tortillas with some additional salsa on the side.

Nutritional value per serving: Calories: 329, Carbs: 54.8 g, Fat: 7.5 g, Protein: 10.6 g.

Spicy Grilled Tofu with Szechuan Vegetables

Preparation Time: 3 minutes

Cooking time: 12 minutes

Servings: 2

Ingredients

1 lb. firm tofu, frozen and thawed

3 tablespoons soy sauce

2 tablespoons toasted sesame oil

2 tablespoons apple cider vinegar

1 clove garlic, minced

1 teaspoon freshly grated ginger

¼ teaspoon red pepper flakes

For the vegetables...

1 tablespoon toasted sesame oil

1 lb. fresh green beans, trimmed

1 red bell pepper, sliced

1 small red onion, sliced

1 teaspoon soy sauce

2 tablespoons Szechuan sauce

1 teaspoon corn starch

Directions:

Start by cutting the tofu into ½" slices then place into a shallow baking dish.

Take a small bowl and add the marinade ingredients. Stir well then pour over the tofu.

Put in a refrigerator for at least 30 minutes.

Preheat the broiler to medium then grill the tofu until firm.

Fill a pot with water and pop over medium heat.

Bring to the boil then add the beans.

Blanche for 2 minutes then drain and rinse.

Take a small bowl and add the corn starch and a teaspoon of cold water.

Place a skillet over medium heat, add the oil then add the beans, red peppers and onions. Stir well.

Add the soy sauce and Szechuan sauce and cook for another minute.

Add the corn starch mixture and stir again.

Serve the veggies and the tofu together.

Nutritional value per serving: Calories: 297, Carbs: 9g, Fat: 20g, Protein: 24g

Vegan-Friendly Fajitas

Preparation Time: 30 minutes
Cooking time: 19 minutes
Servings: 6

Ingredients:

1 cup dry black beans

1 large green bell pepper, seeded, diced

1 poblano pepper, seeded, thinly sliced

1 large avocado, peeled, pitted, mashed

1 medium sweet onion, chopped

3 large portobello mushrooms

2 tbsp. olive oil

6 tortilla wraps

1 tsp. lime juice

1 tsp. chilli powder

1 tsp. garlic powder

¼ tsp. cayenne pepper

Salt to taste

Directions:

Cook the black beans as recommended.

Heat 1 tablespoon of olive oil in a large frying pan over high heat.

Add the bell peppers, poblano peppers, and half of the onions.

Mix in the chilli powder, garlic powder, and cayenne pepper; add salt to taste.

Cook the vegetables until tender and browned, around 10 minutes.

Add the black beans and continue cooking for an additional 2 minutes; then remove the frying pan from the stove.

Add the portobello mushrooms to the skillet and turn the heat down to low. Sprinkle the mushrooms with salt.

Stir/flip the ingredients often and cook until the mushrooms have shrunk down to half their size, around 7 minutes. Remove the frying pan from the heat.

Mix the avocado, remaining 1 tablespoon of olive oil, and the remaining onions together in a small bowl to make a simple guacamole. Stir the lime juice in and add salt and pepper to taste.Spread the guacamole on a tortilla with a spoon and then top with a generous scoop of the mushroom mixture.Serve and enjoy right away, or, allow the prepared tortillas to cool down and wrap them in paper towels to store!

Nutritional value per serving: Calories: 264, Carbs: 27.7 g, Fat: 14 g. Protein: 6.8 g

Incredibly Tasty Pizza

Preparation time: 1 hour and 10 minutes

Cooking time: 1 hour and 45 minutes

Servings: 3

Ingredients:

For the dough:

½ Teaspoon italian seasoning

1 and ½ cups whole wheat flour

1 and ½ teaspoons instant yeast

1 tablespoon olive oil

A pinch of salt

½ Cup warm water

Cooking spray

For the sauce:

¼ Cup green olives, pitted and sliced

¼ Cup kalamata olives, pitted and sliced

½ Cup tomatoes, crushed

1 tablespoon parsley, chopped

1 tablespoon capers, rinsed

¼ Teaspoon garlic powder

¼ Teaspoon basil, dried

¼ Teaspoon oregano, dried

¼ Teaspoon palm sugar

¼ Teaspoon red pepper flakes

A pinch of salt and black pepper

½ Cup cashew mozzarella, shredded

Directions:

In your food processor, mix yeast with italian seasoning, a pinch of salt and flour.Add oil and the water and blend well until you obtain a dough.Transfer dough to a floured working surface, knead well, transfer to a greased bowl, cover and leave aside for 1 hour.Meanwhile, in a bowl, mix green olives with kalamata olives, tomatoes, parsley, capers, garlic powder, oregano, sugar, salt, pepper and pepper flakes and stir well.Transfer pizza dough to a working surface again and flatten it.Shape so it will fit your slow cooker.Grease your slow cooker with cooking spray and add dough.

Press well on the bottom.Spread the sauce mix all over, cover and cook on high for 1 hour and 15 minutes.Spread vegan mozzarella all over, cover again and cook on high for 30 minutes more.Leave your pizza to cool down before slicing and serving it.

Nutrition: calories 340, fat 5, fiber 7, carbs 13, protein 15

Rich Beans Soup

Preparation time: 10 minutes

Cooking time: 7 hours

Servings: 4

Ingredients:

1 pound navy beans

1 yellow onion, chopped

4 garlic cloves, crushed, 2 quarts veggie stock

A pinch of sea salt

Black pepper to the taste

2 potatoes, peeled and cubed

2 teaspoons dill, dried

1 cup sun-dried tomatoes, chopped

1 pound carrots, sliced

4 tablespoons parsley, minced

Directions:Put the stock in your slow cooker.Add beans, onion, garlic, potatoes, tomatoes, carrots, dill, salt and pepper, stir, cover and cook on low for 7 hours.Stir your soup, add parsley, divide into bowls and serve.Enjoy!

Nutrition: calories 250, fat 4, fiber 3, carbs 9, protein 10

Delicious Baked Beans

Preparation time: 10 minutes

Cooking time: 12 hours

Servings: 8

Ingredients:

1 pound navy beans, soaked overnight and drained

1 cup maple syrup

1 cup bourbon

1 cup vegan bbq sauce

1 cup palm sugar

¼ Cup ketchup

1 cup water

¼ Cup mustard, ¼ Cup blackstrap molasses

¼ Cup apple cider vinegar, ¼ Cup olive oil

2 tablespoons coconut aminos

Directions: Put the beans in your slow cooker.Add maple syrup, bourbon, bbq sauce, sugar, ketchup, water, mustard, molasses, vinegar, oil and coconut aminos.Stir everything, cover and cook on Low for 12 hours.Divide into bowls and serve.Enjoy!

Nutrition: calories 430, fat 7, fiber 8, carbs 15, protein 19

Indian Lentils

Preparation time: 10 minutes

Cooking time: 3 hours

Servings: 4

Ingredients:

1 yellow bell pepper, chopped

1 sweet potato, chopped

2 and ½ cups lentils, already cooked

4 garlic cloves, minced

1 yellow onion, chopped

2 teaspoons cumin, ground

15 ounces canned tomato sauce

½ Teaspoon ginger, ground

A pinch of cayenne pepper

1 tablespoons coriander, ground

1 teaspoon turmeric, ground

2 teaspoons paprika

2/3 cup veggie stock

1 teaspoon garam masala

A pinch of sea salt

Black pepper to the taste

Juice of 1 lemon

Directions:

Put the stock in your slow cooker.

Add potato, lentils, onion, garlic, cumin, bell pepper, tomato sauce, salt, pepper, ginger, coriander, turmeric, paprika, cayenne, garam masala and lemon juice.

Stir, cover and cook on high for 3 hours.

Stir your lentils mix again, divide into bowls and serve.

Enjoy!

Nutrition: calories 300, fat 6, fiber 5, carbs 9, protein 12

Delicious Butternut Squash Soup

Preparation time: 10 minutes

Cooking time: 6 hours

Servings: 8

Ingredients:

1 apple, cored, peeled and chopped

½ Pound carrots, chopped

1 pound butternut squash, peeled and cubed

1 yellow onion, chopped

A pinch of sea salt

Black pepper to the taste

1 bay leaf

3 cups veggie stock

14 ounces canned coconut milk

¼ Teaspoon sage, dried

Directions:Put the stock in your slow cooker.Add apple squash, carrots, onion, salt, pepper and bay leaf.Stir, cover and cook on low for 6 hours.Transfer to your blender, add coconut milk and sage and pulse really well.Ladle into bowls and serve right away.Enjoy!

Nutrition: calories 200, fat 3, fiber 6, carbs 8, protein 10

Chapter 12. Dinner Recipes

Black Bean and Veggie Soup

Servings: 6

Calories: 308

Preparation Time: 10 minutes

Cooking Time: 45 minutes

Ingredients

Olive oil - 2 tablespoons

Onion (diced) - 1

Celery stalks (chopped) - 2

Carrot (chopped) - 1

Red bell pepper (diced) - 1

Garlic (minced) - 4 cloves

Jalapeño (seeded and diced) - 1

Salt - 1 teaspoon

Pepper - 1 teaspoon

Cumin - 2 tablespoons

Black beans (drained and rinsed) – 4 cans (60 ounces)

Vegetable stock - 4 cups

Bay leaf – 1

For serving

Avocado (chopped)

Queso fresco (crumbled)

Fresh cilantro (chopped)

Tortilla chip (crumbled)

Nutrition:

Fat: 6 g

Carbohydrates: 49 g

Protein: 17 g

Directions

Start by taking a stock-pot (large) and place it over high flame. Add in the oil and reduce the heat the medium–high.

Once the oil starts to shimmer, toss in the onions, carrot, bell peppers and celery.

Let the veggies cook for about 5 minutes. Keep stirring.

Now add in the minced garlic, pepper and salt. Cook for about 10 more minutes. The veggies should be tender by now.

Add in the vegetable stock, black beans, bay leaf and cumin.

Bring the ingredients to a boil and reduce the flame to low. Cover the stock-pot with a lid and cook for about 30 minutes. Beans should also be tender by now.

Take a blender and transfer 4 cups of the beans and vegetable soup into the same. Blend into a smooth puree like consistency.

Pour the blended vegetables and beans into the stock-pot. Mix well to combine. This will help in thickening the soup.

Let the soup simmer over low flame for another 10 minutes.

Once done, garnish with queso fresco, avocado, tortilla chips and chopped cilantro.

Vegetable and Tofu Skewers

Servings: 4

Calories: 187

Preparation Time: 10 minutes (1 hour additional)

Cooking Time: 17 minutes

Ingredients

Water - ½ cup

Maple syrup - ¼ cup

Soy sauce - 3 tablespoons

BBQ sauce - 2 tablespoons

Oil - 1 tablespoon

Garlic powder - 1 tablespoon

Sriracha - 1 tablespoon

Black pepper - 1 teaspoon

Firm tofu - 15 ounces

Peppers - 2

Onions – 2 medium

Zucchini - 1

Skewers - 4

Nutrition:

Fat: 9 g

Carbohydrates: 17 g

Protein: 11 g

Directions

Start by taking a shallow dish and fill it with water. Soak the wooden skewers in the same as this will prevent them from burning.

Take the zucchini and slice it in round slices. Also cut peppers and onions in squares.

In the meanwhile, take a quarter plate and line it with a paper towel. Place tofu and cover it with another paper towel and place a plate on top.

Place the tofu along with plates in the microwave for about 3 minutes.

Remove the tofu and place it on a chopping board. Cut it into cubes.

Take a glass measuring cup and add in the water, soy sauce, maple syrup, oil, barbeque sauce, pepper, Sriracha and garlic powder. Stir well.

Take a rectangle storage box and place the tofu inside it. Pour the prepared sauce over tofu and cover it with a lid. Place it in the refrigerator for about an hour.

Once done, remove the tofu from marinade. Keep aside

Take a non-stick saucepan and pour the marinating liquid to the saucepan. Place it over low flame for about 10 minutes. Put off the flame once the sauce starts to thicken.

Remove the skewers from the water and start assembling them.

Take 1 skewer and start assembling by alternating between zucchini, onion, pepper and tofu.

Take a grill pan and place in medium flame. Cook each assembled skewer on each side for about 4 minutes. Glaze each side with sauce while cooking.

All sides should have a light char as this will add nice smoky flavor to the dish.

Vegan Alfredo Fettuccine Pasta

Servings: 2

Calories: 844

Preparation Time: 15 minutes

Cooking Time: 15 minutes

Ingredients

White potatoes - 2 medium

White onion - ¼

Italian seasoning - 1 tablespoon

Lemon juice - 1 teaspoon

Garlic - 2 cloves

Salt - 1 teaspoon

Fettuccine pasta - 12 ounces

Raw cashew - ½ cup

Nutritional yeast (optional) - 1 teaspoon

Truffle oil (optional) - ¼ teaspoon

Nutrition:

Fat: 13 g

Carbohydrates: 152 g

Protein: 28 g

Directions

Start by placing a pot on high flame and boiling 4 cups of water.

Peel the potatoes and cut them into small cubes. Cut the onion into cubes as well.

Add the potatoes and onions to the boiling water and cook for about 10 minutes.

Remove the onions and potatoes. Keep aside. Save the water.

Take another pot and fill it with water. Season generously with salt.

Toss in the fettuccine pasta and cook as per package instructions.

Take a blender and add in the raw cashews, veggies, nutritional yeast, truffle oil, lemon juice and 1 cup of saved water. Blend into a smooth puree.

Add in the garlic and salt.

Drain the cooked pasta using a colander. Transfer into a mixing bowl.

Pour the prepared sauce on top of the cooked fettuccine pasta. Serve.

Spinach Pasta in Pesto Sauce

Servings: 2

Calories: 591

Preparation Time: 20 minutes

Cooking Time: 15 minutes

Ingredients

Olive oil - 1 tablespoon

Spinach - 5 ounces

All-purpose flour - 2 cups

Salt - 1 tablespoon plus ¼ teaspoon (keep it divided)

Water - 2 tablespoons

Roasted vegetable for serving

Pesto for serving

Fresh basil for serving

Nutrition:

Fat: 8 g

Carbohydrates: 110 g

Protein: 16 g

Directions

Take a large pot and fill it with water. Place it over high flame and bring the water to a boil. Add one tablespoon of salt

While the water is boiling, place a large saucepan over medium flame. Pour in the olive oil and heat it through.

Once the oil starts to shimmer, toss in the spinach and sauté for 5 minutes.

Take a food processor and transfer the wilted spinach. Process until the spinach is fine in texture.

Add in the flour bit by bit and continue to process to form a crumbly dough.

Further, add ¼ tsp of salt and 1 tbsp of water while processing to bring the dough together. Add the remaining 1 tbsp of water if required.

Remove the dough onto a flat surface and sprinkle with flour. Knead well to form a dough ball.Use a rolling pin to roll out the dough. The dimensions of the rolled dough should be 18 inches long and 12 inches wide. The thickness should be about ¼ - inch thick.Cut the rolled dough into long and even strips using a pizza cutter. Make sure the strips are ½ - inch wide. The strips need to be rolled into evenly sized thick noodles.Toss in the prepared noodles and cook for about 4 minutes. Drain using a colander.Transfer the noodles into a large mixing bowl and add in the roasted vegetables, pesto. Toss well to combine.Garnish with basil leaves.

No Meat Sloppy Joes

Servings: 4

Calories: 451

Preparation Time: 10 minutes

Cooking Time: 24 minutes

Ingredients

Olive oil – ½ teaspoon

Yellow onion (diced) - ½ medium

Green capsicum (diced) - ½

Garlic (minced) - 2 cloves

Chili powder - ½ teaspoon

Cumin - ½ teaspoon

Paprika - ½ teaspoon

Salt – as per taste

Textured vegetable protein - 1 cup

Vegetable broth - 1 cup

Tomato sauce - 1 can (15 ounces)

Vegan Worcestershire sauce - 1 teaspoon

Soy sauce - 1 tablespoon

Brown sugar - 1 teaspoon

Yellow mustard - 2 teaspoons

Hamburger buns - 4

Nutrition:

Fat: 10 g

Carbohydrates: 61 g

Protein: 27 g

Directions

Start by taking a medium-sized skillet and place it over medium flame. Pour olive oil and heat through.

Once the oil is heated, add in the diced onions and sauté for 3 minutes.

Now toss in the diced capsicum and sauté for 3 more minutes.

Add in the garlic, cumin, chili powder, salt and paprika and sauté for another 3 minutes.

Add in the vegetable protein, tomato sauce and vegetable broth. Stir well to combine. Cover with a lid and let it cook for about 15 minutes.

Open the lid and keep on the side. Add in the soy sauce, Worcestershire sauce, yellow mustard and brown sugar. Mix well. Cook for about 4 minutes. Place the prepared mixture between the hamburger buns and serve hot!

Acorn Squash Stuffed with Veggies and Wild Rice

Servings: 2

Calories: 409

Preparation Time: 10 minutes

Cooking Time: 1 hour 40 minutes

Ingredients

Acorn squashes - 2

Olive oil - 1 tablespoon (some extra)

Salt – as per taste

Pepper – as per taste

Wild rice (rinsed) - ¾ cup

Vegetable broth - 1 ¼ cups (2 tablespoons extra, divided)

Chili powder - ½ teaspoon

Ground cumin - ¼ teaspoon

Maple syrup - 1 ½ teaspoon

Cremini mushroom (sliced) - 5 ounces

Shiitake mushroom (sliced) – 5 ounces

Onion (chopped) - ½ medium

Garlic (minced) - 2 cloves

Fresh rosemary (chopped) - 1 teaspoon

Fresh thyme (chopped) - 1 teaspoon

White wine - ¼ cup

Kale (chopped) - 2 cups

Pomegranate seeds - 2 tablespoons

Nutrition:

Fat: 5 g

Carbohydrates: 88 g

Protein: 13 g

Directions

Start by preheating the oven by setting the temperature to 375 degrees Fahrenheit.

Place the squash on the chopping board and cut in half from stem side up. Remove the seeds and keep aside. Scoop out the pulp into a bowl and keep aside.

Place the squash on a baking tray with cut-side facing up. Brush the squash with oil and evenly sprinkle with pepper and salt.

Transfer into the oven and bake for about 40 minutes.

While the squash is cooking, take a small stockpot and add in 1 ¼ cups of vegetable broth. Let it come to a boil. Cover using a lid and let it simmer for about 45 minutes over low flame.

Place the squash seeds in a strainer and rinse them thoroughly. Dry them using a dishtowel.

Transfer the seeds into a small bowl. Add in the cumin, chili powder, maple syrup and salt. Toss well to until all seeds are evenly coated.

Remove the baking tray from the oven and shift the squash to one side. Make a shallow tray using the parchment paper. Place the seeds in the same and transfer back into the oven.

Bake for about 15 minutes. The squash should be tender and seeds should be crispy.

Take a large skillet and add in the olive oil. Place it over medium flame.

Once the oil is heated through, toss in the mushrooms and sauté for about 8 minutes.

Toss in the onions and sauté for about 4 minutes. Further, drizzle some olive oil and add in the rosemary, thyme and garlic. Cook for about 4 minutes. Pour in the white wine to deglaze the skillet. Cook for about 2 minutes. Add in the kale, pepper and salt. Sauté until kale starts wilting and reduces to a quarter of the volume. Add in the wild rice and mix through. Remove the skillet from the flame and keep aside.

Place both squashes on serving platter and fill them with kale and mushroom mixture. Garnish with pomegranate seeds and crispy squash seeds.

Tofu Turkey and Drumsticks

Servings: 6

Calories: 339

Preparation Time: 20 minutes

Cooking Time: 1 hour

Ingredients

Extra-firm tofu - 14 ounces

Pinto bean - ¾ cup

Nutritional yeast - 6 tablespoons

Soy sauce - ¼ cup

Poultry seasoning - 1 tablespoon

Garlic (chopped) - 3 cloves

Kosher salt - ½ teaspoon

Pepper - 1 teaspoon

Onion powder - 1 teaspoon

Vegetable broth (low sodium) - 1 cup

Olive oil - 2 tablespoons

Vital wheat gluten - 2 ½ cups

Vegan stuffing - ½ cup

Wooden skewers – 2

Gravy (of choice) - for serving

Nutrition:

Fat: 9 g

Carbohydrates: 18 g

Protein: 47 g

Directions

Start by preheating the oven by setting the temperature to 375 degrees Fahrenheit.

Take a shallow dish and fill it with water. Soak the skewers in the same.

Take a medium-sized bowl and line it with a kitchen towel. Crumble the tofu in the bowl. Gather all the edges of the kitchen towel and press through the center to squeeze out excess liquid.

Take a food processor and add in the drained tofu, pinto beans, soy sauce, nutritional yeast, onion powder, poultry seasoning, pepper, salt, vegetable broth and onion powder. Blend into a smooth puree like consistency. While the processor is running, add in the olive oil. Make sure all ingredients are well incorporated.

Take a large bowl and add in the wheat gluten. Now transfer the prepared puree from the food processor to the same bowl. Stir well to combine all the ingredients together. Knead into a smooth dough and transfer onto a flat surface. Form a ball.

Cut out a quarter of the dough and keep aside.

Place the rest of the dough into a glass bowl. Make a well into the center by stretching the edges. It needs to be expanded to about 4 inches in diameter.

Place the vegetable stuffing in the well and enclose the well by stretching the edges.

Take a parchment paper and nicely wrap the dough. Also, wrap the dough in a foil.

Take the saved dough and divide in two equal halves. Form the dough in the shape of drumsticks. Insert soaked skewers in both the drumsticks. Wrap both the drumsticks nice with parchment paper and then in foil. Enclose the edges nicely.

Take a baking tray and place both drumsticks and tofu turkey. Bake for about 20 minutes and flip over. Bake for another 20 minutes and flip over again. Remove the drumsticks after 40 minutes.

Bake the tofu turkey for 20 more minutes.

Once done, remove from the oven and transfer the drumsticks and tofu turkey onto a wooden chopping block. Remove the foil and parchment paper.

Place onto a serving platter and serve with your choice of gravy.

Chapter 13. Snacks And Salad Recipes

Energy Bars

Preparation Time: 5 minutes

Cooking Time: 20 minutes

Servings: Makes 12 bars

Ingredients:

½ cup raisins

1 cup desiccated coconut

1 tsp. vanilla extract

½ cup hemp seeds, shelled

1 tsp. cinnamon, ground

½ cup sesame seeds

4 tbsp. maple syrup

½ cup pumpkin seeds

½ cup cashew butter or any nut butter

1 ½ cup mixed nuts, chopped

1 tsp. vanilla extract

Directions:

First preheat the oven to 350°F.

Mix the coconut, cinnamon, nuts and raisin in a medium-sized mixing bowl.

Add the cashew butter and maple syrup to a small saucepan and heat it over medium heat until melted and smooth.

Stir in the vanilla extract.

Pour the cashew butter mixture into the mixing bowl and stir until everything comes together. Tip: Add water if needed to help the mixture come together.

Transfer the mixture to a greased baking tin and press it down into the tin so it is evenly spread.

Bake for 13 to 15 minutes or until golden brown.

Allow the bars to cool completely and slice them into bars. Store in an air-tight container.

Tip: You can add toppings like walnuts and pecan.

Nutrition:

Calories: 340Kcal

Protein: 10g

Carbohydrates: 20.8g

Fat: 24.4g

Vegan Muffins

Preparation Time: 5 minutes

Cooking Time: 25 minutes

Servings: 6

Ingredients:

1 oz. protein powder

1 tsp. baking powder

2 tbsp. pumpkin seeds

2 tbsp. dried cherries

1 cup oats

1 tbsp. sesame seeds, roasted

For the wet ingredients:

3 tbsp. olive oil

½ cup almond milk

1/2 cup apple sauce

Directions:

Preheat the oven to 390°F.

Combine all the dry ingredients into a large mixing bowl until mixed well.

Next, mix all the wet ingredients in another bowl and combine well.

Pour the wet ingredients into the dry and whisk until everything comes together.

Transfer the mixture to a greased and lined baking dish.

Finally, bake for 28 to 30 minutes or until they are golden brown.

Cool the muffins on the rack, then enjoy.

Tip: You could top the muffins with pumpkin seeds for a crunchy topping.

Nutrition:

Calories: 244Kcal

Protein: 11g

Carbohydrates: 24g

Fat: 13g

Cacao Walnut Balls

Preparation Time: 5 minutes

Cooking Time: 25 minutes

Servings: 6

Ingredients:

1 cup quinoa flour

1 cup walnut, halved

½ cup coconut flakes

3 tbsp. cacao powder

1 oz. protein powder, unflavored

1 cup coconut flakes

Pinch of sea salt

¼ cup dried apricots, chopped thinly

Directions:

Place all the ingredients, apart from the coconut flakes, into a large mixing bowl. Once everything is well combined, shape pieces of the mixture into balls and then coat each ball with coconut flakes.

Finally, place the balls in the refrigerator for a few hours and serve them chilled.

Tip: These balls are freezer friendly and can stay frozen for up to 2 months.

Nutrition: Calories: 343Kcal Protein: 12g Carbohydrates: 26g Fat: 24g

Almond Oats Energy Balls

Preparation Time: 5 minutes

Cooking Time: 25 minutes

Servings: 8

Ingredients:

½ cup almonds, roasted & crushed

1 cup oats

½ cup coconut milk

2 medium bananas

2 oz. protein powder

2 tbsp. chia seeds

1 tsp. cinnamon, ground

2 tbsp. cocoa or coconut flakes

Directions:

Combine the chia seeds and coconut milk in a large mixing bowl.

Set aside for 5 minutes and then stir in the rest of the ingredients. Mix well.

Transfer the mixture to a high-speed blender. Blend for ½ minutes or until it is just combined.

Put the mixture into the freezer for 10 minutes to chill it.

Next, shape the mixture into balls and dip them in cocoa powder.

Serve them chilled.

Tip: If you prefer, you can use your choice of low-carb sweetener.

Nutrition: Calories: 224Kcal Protein: 13g Carbohydrates: 24g Fat: 10g

Spicy Chickpeas

Preparation Time: 10 minutes

Cooking Time: 35 minutes

Servings: 6

Ingredients:

¼ cup olive oil

½ tsp. cayenne pepper

2 × 15 oz. chickpeas

¾ tsp. paprika

1 tsp. sea salt

½ tsp. chili powder

½ tsp. onion powder

½ tsp. cumin

Sea salt, as needed

¾ tsp. garlic powder

Directions: Preheat the oven to 425°F. Drain the chickpeas and let them dry in a towel-lined dish for 10 to 15 minutes.Transfer the chickpeas onto a lined baking sheet and spread them out in a single layer .Drizzle olive oil over the chickpeas and sprinkle with salt. Bake them in the oven for 23 to 25 minutes or until they are golden brown, stirring frequently. Once baked, stir in the remaining spices and toss well. Next, season and taste, adding more salt and pepper as needed. Serve and enjoy.Tip: You can also reduce the quantity of cayenne pepper to ¼ tsp.

Nutrition: Calories: 224Kcal Protein: 13g Carbohydrates: 24g Fat: 10g

Peanut Butter Cups

Preparation Time: 10 minutes

Cooking Time: 35 minutes

Servings: 9

Ingredients:

2 tsp. coconut oil

1 cup peanut butter, creamy

10 0z. vegan, sugar-free chocolate chips

3 scoops chocolate protein powder

2 tbsp. maple syrup

Directions:

To begin, combine the peanut butter, protein powder and maple syrup in a large mixing bowl until mixed well.

Next, place the coconut oil and chocolate chips in a microwave-safe bowl and melt the mixture by heating it on a high heat.

Spoon the chocolate mixture into the bottom of the greased baking cups.

Add the peanut butter mixture on top of the chocolate mixture.

Finally, add the remaining chocolate on top of the peanut butter.

Place them in the refrigerator until set.

Serve and enjoy.

Tip: Make sure to add organic coconut oil.

Nutrition: Calories: 341Kcal Protein: 11.6g Carbohydrates: 30.4g Fat: 22.4g

Coleslaw Pasta Salad

Preparation Time: 5 minutes

Cooking Time: 30 minutes

Servings: 4

Ingredients:

4 scallions, sliced thinly

10 oz. pasta

1 lb. carrot, shredded

1 lb. white cabbage, shredded

For the dressing:

1 tsp. sea salt

½ cup vegan mayonnaise

1/2 tsp. black pepper, ground

2 tbsp. maple syrup

½ cup hummus

Juice of ½ of 1 lemon

2 tbsp. dijon mustard

Directions: Start by cooking the pasta, following the instructions given in the packet. Cook until al dente then drain. After that, make the dressing by placing all the ingredients in a medium bowl until combined well. Add the pasta along with the remaining ingredients. Spoon the dressing over it and toss well. Serve and enjoy.

Tip: You could add nuts like walnuts to it to make the salad more nutritious.

Nutrition: Calories: 524Kcal Protein: 17g Carbohydrates: 85g Fat: 14g

Corn Avocado Salad

Preparation Time: 10 minutes

Cooking Time: 15 minutes

Servings: 4

Ingredients:

1 cup frozen edamame, unshelled, 2 avocadoes, sliced

1 medium shallot, sliced thinly

2 cups cherry tomatoes, halved

2 cups sweet corn kernels, frozen

For the dressing:

Juice of 1 lime

¼ tsp. chili powder

1 tsp. sea salt

1 tsp. extra virgin olive oil

¼ cup fresh cilantro, sliced thinly

Directions: Boil water in a medium-sized saucepan over a medium-high heat. Once it starts boiling, stir in the corn and simmer them for 6 to 8 minutes or until cooked.

Tip: Make sure to not overcook. Drain. Transfer to a large mixing bowl and allow it to cool. Mix all the dressing ingredients in another bowl until combined well. Then add the rest of the ingredients along with dressing to the mixing bowl and toss well. Taste for seasoning and add more salt and pepper if needed. Serve and enjoy. Tip: Pair it with toasted whole-grain bread.

Nutrition: Calories: 375Kcal Protein: 14g Carbohydrates: 43g Fat: 20g

Couscous with Chickpeas Salad

Preparation Time: 10 minutes

Cooking Time: 15 minutes

Servings: 4

Ingredients:

For the couscous:

1 cup couscous
1 ½ cup water
For the salad:

12 oz. tofu, extra-firm
1 medium shallot, sliced thinly
1 cup chickpeas, washed
½ tsp. turmeric powder
1 tbsp. olive oil
1 cucumber, diced
½ tsp. turmeric powder
1 cucumber, diced
4 tbsp. pine nuts
1 cup dill
For the dressing:

Dash of pepper, ground

1 tbsp. dijon mustard

1 tsp. sea salt

½ cup orange juice

Directions:

Boil water in a pot over medium-high heat.

When it starts boiling, pour the hot water to a large heatproof bowl with couscous in it.

Cover the heatproof bowl with a lid and allow it to sit for 10 to 15 minutes or until all the liquid is absorbed.

Fluff the couscous with a fork.

Heat a skillet and spoon in 1/3 of the oil into it.

Then, stir in the sliced shallot and cook them for 3 minutes or until transparent. Set aside on a plate.

Add tofu to the skillet along with the remaining oil.

Fry the tofu for 8 to 10 minutes or until they are golden brown.

To this, add the turmeric powder and mix again.

In another bowl, stir in all the dressing ingredients until combined.

Finally, combine the couscous, salad ingredients and dressing in a large mixing bowl until mixed well.

Tip: Add a squeeze of lemon juice over as a finishing touch.

Nutrition:

Calories: 408Kcal

Protein: 18g

Carbohydrates: 54g

Fat: 14g

Black & White Bean Salad

Preparation Time: 10 minutes

Cooking Time: 15 minutes

Servings: 4

Ingredients:

For the salad:

¼ cup red onion, chopped

1/3 cup quinoa

1 cup cucumber, sliced

19 oz. drained black beans, washed

1 jalapeno pepper, seeded and minced

19 oz. drained navy beans, washed

¼ cup fresh coriander, chopped

For the dressing:

¼ tsp. pepper

¼ cup vegetable oil

¼ tsp. salt

2 tbsp. lime juice

½ tsp. chili powder

1 tsp. coriander, ground

1 tbsp. cider vinegar

½ tsp. oregano, dried

1 garlic clove, minced

Directions:

Cook the quinoa for 10 to 12 minutes in a deep saucepan filled with ¾ cup of water until it becomes tender.

Make the dressing by combining all the dressing ingredients in a small bowl until mixed well.

Finally, add all the salad ingredients to a large mixing bowl and stir in the cooked quinoa and dressing. Toss well.

Serve and enjoy.

Tip: Try adding tomato to the recipe.

Nutrition:

Calories: 573Kcal

Protein: 26.7g

Carbohydrates: 83.5g

Fat: 16.3g

Quinoa with Apple & Kale

Preparation Time: 10 minutes

Cooking Time: 25 minutes

Servings: 3

Ingredients:

5 cups kale

1 cup quinoa, washed

2 cloves of garlic, minced

1 tbsp. lemon juice

2 cups vegetable stock

Salt and pepper, as needed

2 tbsp. extra virgin olive oil

1 tbsp. coconut oil

1 tbsp. dijon mustard

1 large apple, diced

2 tbsp. maple syrup

3 tbsp. water

2 tbsp. apple cider vinegar

Chapter 14. Smoothies Recipes

Greens and Chocolate Protein Shake

Preparation Time: 70 minutes

Servings: 1

Ingredients:

¾ cup almond milk

2 large dates, pitted

1 tables poon cocoa powder

A pinch ground cinnamon

½ cup frozen organic kale

1 tablespoon hemp seeds, hulled

1 medium banana, sliced, frozen

1/8 cup chopped avocado

Ice cubes, as required

Directions:

Add all the ingredients into a blender. Blend for 30 – 40 seconds or until smooth. Pour into a glass and serve.

Nutrition: Calories: 250 Fat: 9 g
Carbohydrate: 38 g,Fiber: 8 g Protein: 10 g

Chocolate Black Bean Smoothie

Preparation Time: 40 minutes

Ingredients:

2 bananas, sliced, frozen

1 cup cooked black beans

2 cups almond milk or any other nondairy milk of your choice

2 tablespoons cocoa powder

2 cups frozen cauliflower

4 medjool dates, pitted, chopped

2 tablespoons hemp seeds

2 teaspoons ground cinnamon

To garnish:

Cocoa nibs (optional)

Directions:

Add all the ingredients into a blender. Blend for 30 – 40 seconds or until smooth.

Pour into 2 large glasses. Garnish with cocoa nibs and serve.

Nutrition: 2 large glasses Nutrition:
Calories: 452 Fat: 11 g Carbohydrate: 77 g, Fiber: 18 g Protein: 19 g

Peanut Butter Protein Smoothie

Preparation Time: 30 minutes

Servings: 1

Ingredients:

1 cup torn kale (discard hard stems and ribs)

1 tablespoon hemp seeds

1/3 cup water

½ cup almond milk or cashew milk

½ scoop vegan vanilla protein powder

½ banana, sliced

½ tablespoon peanut butter

1 cup ice

1 tablespoon cacao powder

Directions:

First add kale into the blender followed by banana, hemp seeds and peanut butter.

Add ice, water and almond milk and blend until smooth. Add rest of the ingredients and blend until smooth. Pour into a tall glass and serve.

Nutrition: Calories: 286 Fat: 11.6 g Carbohydrate: 27.9 g,

 Fiber: 6 g Protein: 16.8 g

Peanut Butter, Jelly and Date Smoothie

Preparation Time: 20 minutes

Servings: 2

Ingredients:

8 dates, pitted

2 medium bananas, sliced, frozen

2/3 cup blueberries

2 tablespoons natural peanut butter

1 ½ cups vanilla almond milk, unsweetened

2 tablespoons flaxseed meal

Directions:

Place all the ingredients into a blender. Blend for 30 – 40 seconds or until smooth.

Pour into 2 glasses and serve.

Nutrition:

Calories: 374

Fat: 13 g Carbohydrate: 60 g,

 Fiber: 11 g Protein: 8 g

Berry and Oatmeal Smoothie

Preparation Time: 20 minutes

Servings: 2 large glasses

Ingredients:

2 cups frozen strawberries

2 cups frozen blueberries

4 tablespoons maple syrup

4 tablespoons almond butter

2 inches fresh ginger, peeled, chopped

4 cups baby spinach

2 cups wate

6 tablespoons hulled hemp seeds

½ cup rolled oats

Directions:

Place all the ingredients into a blender. Blend for 30 – 40 seconds or until smooth.

Pour into 2 large glasses and serve.

Nutrition: Calories: 680

Fat: 36 g Carbohydrate: 84 g, Fiber: NA Protein: 21 g

Vanilla Clementine Protein Smoothie

Preparation Time: 70 minutes

Servings: 2

Ingredients:

6 clementine's, peeled, separated into segments, deseeded

2 cups light vanilla soymilk

16 almonds

1 scoop vegan vanilla protein powder

2 tablespoons flaxseed meal

Ice cubes, as required

Directions:

Place all the ingredients into a blender. Blend for 30 – 40 seconds or until smooth.

Pour into 2 glasses and serve.

Nutrition:

Calories: 336

Fat: 11.1 g

Carbohydrate: 39.8 g,

Fiber: 9.1 g

Protein: 27.3 g

Chapter 15. Don't Forget To Exercise

There are several things that you can do in order to meet your weight loss goals. These include cutting back on the number of calories that you eat each day and starting a healthy exercise program are two great ways to meet your goals, especially if you combine them both together. It is still important to maintain an exercise program even after you have reached your weight loss goals in order to maintain the weight loss. After you have decided to go on a diet and start an exercise program the first thing that you will be asking yourself is how much exercise that you will need.

An important step that you should consider doing before you start any exercise plan is to talk to your doctor. They will be able to tell you if the plan is good for you, how much exercise you should do, and give you any advice and suggestions about what will work in your situation. They will also be able to do a complete checkup in order to make sure that they are no underlying problems in your health that could affect what types of exercises you are able to do.

You should consider some basic considerations when you start a diet. It is important to remember that there are no magic pills or amazing diet plans that will help you to lose the weigh overnight. Even if you do lose a lot of weight quickly on a particular plan, it is not likely that you will be able to keep the weight off for the long term.

The easiest and safest way to lose weight is to combine exercise and a good diet together. However, there are certain amounts of exercise that you should meat in order to either lose the weight or maintain a healthy weight. Before you start you should remember that the way to lose one pound of fat is by consuming 3500 less calories in your diet. This means that if you want to lose a pound a week then you will need to burn at least 500 calories a day. You can cut either these calories out by eating less, exercising more, or doing a combination of both.

There are no magic exercise plans that work for everyone and help everyone to lose the weight. Each person has a different body and responds in different ways to certain types of exercise. It might take some trial and error in order to find out which exercises that you enjoy and which ones work the best for you.

If you are looking to exercise to lose weight there are some guidelines that you should follow. It is recommended by the Centers for Disease Control and Prevention that you try to get at least two hours and 30 minutes of exercise in a week in order to lose weight. This might sound like a lot but it ends up only being about 30 minutes five days a week; of course, the more exercise that you do, the greater the results of the weight loss. You will have to incorporate more exercise into your routine if you do not plan to cut back on your calories in order to see weight loss.

Some activities that you should include in your exercise plan include cardiovascular exercises such as walking, running, biking, hiking and swimming. In order to burn the largest amount of calories during your workout you need to elevate your heart rate and keep it at that rate for an extended time during the workout.

It is not a good idea to spend all of your time concentrating on aerobic exercises. While they are great for your heart and in helping you to burn calories and lose weight, you should include also other activities in your work out. These include strength training and stretching exercises, which can help make your bones and muscles stronger and help slim your waistline.

You can get just so many benefits from exercising. One of the benefits includes weight loss. Just for spending an hour doing a low impact exercise a 160 pound person can lose somewhere around 350 calories. If you decide to do a higher impact activity such as running you could lose up to 900 calories in that hour, which is way more than you need to burn in order to lose a pound per week.

Just how much exercise that you need in your exercise program will depend on how much weight you will want to lose? If you live a very sedentary life, and you want to lose a lot of weight, you will have to include more exercise in your day than someone who has a job that keeps them moving all day. It is a good idea to start with 30 minutes a couple of times a day and slowly build up to working out between 30-60 minutes at least five days a week.

Tips to Keep Motivated

Staying motivated on an exercise plan can be tough. You might start out with all of the best intentions, but after a few weeks or so, you will get worn out and not want to continue. It is much easier to just sit on the couch and hope that everything works out the way that you would like. While you know all of the great reasons to get up and do some exercising, it just is not as much fun, or at least is more work, than some of the other things you might want to do. Here are some of the best tips that you can use that will help you to keep motivated and get in a great workout every day.

Set some goals

Before you even head out to the gym, make sure that you are setting some goals. Make them challenging enough that you will need to put in some work, but simple enough that you would actually be able to get them done if you work hard. For example, it is not a good idea to say you will lose ten pounds a week, but saying you want to lose 2 pounds is reasonable.

Write down these goals from the beginning. They can be anything that you want as long as they give you a bit of a challenge and make you work for it. You can say that you will lose a certain amount of weight over time, go by the measurements in your body, or you can even choose to go for a specific amount of time or reps. It is up to you, just make sure that you are having some fun and working hard while at the gym.

Bring along music

Getting on the treadmill and staring at a wall for 30 to 60 minutes is going to get boring fast. You might enjoy it the first few times, but after that, the activity is not going to be as much fun and you will find that your motivation starts to slip away. This is why you should consider bringing something along to do while you are working out. This can be almost anything. Many people like to bring along some of their favorite music. This allows them to have something fun and upbeat to listen to while they are working out plus can get them pumped up and in the right mood to keep going.

Do an activity you love

It honestly does not matter how much you think an activity is going to help you to lose weight, if you are not enjoying it, you are less likely to keep up with it and you are not going to lose weight. Find something that you like doing, such as biking, swimming, weight lifting, walking, running, or maybe even a group class, and then do that. Even if it is not burning as many calories as another activity, at least you are having fun. The more fun you have with an activity, the better results you will have because you are more likely to keep going with it.

Try a new activity

It is always good to mix things up when you are at the gym. Even if you love an activity, you might find that after a few months of doing it all of the time, you are getting bored with it. Plus, your body is going to become used to a certain activity and you will not get the same results if you keep doing it. Find a few activities that you enjoy, or try a few new ones, and the switch them around on occasion. This allows you to do something new, continue having fun, and you can continue seeing results all at the same time.

Find a friend

For some people, the way that they get some motivation is to find a friend who is going to work out with them. This person should be someone who is looking for the same goals and who will be able to hold you accountable to show up. When you are doing the work outs on your own, it is easy to say that you'll get to it tomorrow and then you never go back. On the other hand, when you know that someone is waiting at the gym for you, you might feel a bit more obligated to show up. Once there, you might as well get in a good work out since you went to all of the trouble. This means you get in a work out much more often than you would on your own, and the results will be much better.

Get outside

You do not need to spend all of your time inside in the gym. When the weather is nice and you are having some trouble getting to the gym, why not take a good walk outside. This is one of the best ways to get in a good workout and can help to lift up your mood because you are getting plenty of fresh air and sunlight.

Reward yourself

Whenever you are able to reach some of your goals while working out, you should take the time to reward yourself. This allows you to feel good about the hard work you are doing and even gives you something to look forward to. You should not let the award be about food since you are trying to lose weight and this can ruin your plans. But choosing to go out a night with friends, go see a movie, purchase some new clothes, or give yourself a spa day can be great incentives to keep yourself going.

Each person is going to have some of their own methods to use that will motivate them to see success. While it might be hard to get on a good workout program, it is important to find a way to get on one and stick with it for your overall health. Once you get started and do it well for a few weeks, it becomes a routine and is much easier to do. Follow some of the tips in this chapter and see how easy it can be to get in your required work out each day.

The Benefits of Exercising

You have probably heard about it for your whole life. People have been telling you that exercise is important and that you should make sure to get in enough each and every day. But why is it so important to work out? Why can't you just sit on the couch and watch your favorite show instead of hitting the gym and trying to do all of that work. This chapter is going to spend a bit of time discussing the benefits that can come with exercising and why you need to get some in everyday.

Weight Loss

The first reason why many people will choose to exercise and work out is because they are looking to lose weight. Every weight loss and diet plan in the world will spell out how important it is to get in a good exercise program if you really want to lose weight. While limiting your calories can help out a lot, you are only able to limit those so much and exercising can help pick up the slack so that you are able to lose more. Pick a moderate to high intensity work out for the best results.

Heart Health

For you to really get a good workout, you will need to get that heart pumping and working hard. When the heart is functioning at this level, it is becoming stronger than ever before. When you sit on the couch, the heart barely has to move in order to get the nutrients all around the body so it is not becoming very strong. With a good work out that makes you sweat and gets the heart up a bit, you can work on its strength and become stronger in no time.

Brain Functioning

Studies have shown that getting in some exercise during the week is critical if you want your brain to function the way that it is supposed to. Exercise can help increase the flow of oxygen and blood to the brain which opens it up for working so much more efficiently. An added bonus is that exercise can help you out with your memory. This is important for those who are aging and need a bit of help recalling important events and facts. Of course, you may be able to find a lot of benefits of this as a younger person as well when you exercise right before a test and are better able to recall the facts you learn.

Stress

Stress is a daily part of life for most people and there is not much that they can do in order to get it to go away. But there are some things that you can do to reduce the amount of stress that you are feeling and to get yourself to look and feel better about the stress. Any time that the stress is starting to get too much for you, go and do a quick run or pop in your favorite work out movie. This will allow you to take a break from the stress you are feeling and you can better get back on track with other things.

Cholesterol

High cholesterol is a huge problem that a lot of people are dealing with because of the high fat diet found in this country. When you get on a good workout program, you can help to reduce the amount of bad cholesterol that is in the blood while also increasing the kind of good that is there.

Blood Pressure

When eating a diet that is high in sodium, or when you sit on the couch all day and do not perform some kind of physical activity, it is easy for you to get high blood pressure. One of the first things that the doctor is going to recommend that you do is get out and start exercising at least five days a week. This will allow the heart to function properly, your cholesterol to go lower, and your body to be better able to reduce the salts that are in there. All of this combines to allow your blood pressure to go way down.

Diabetes

Even the symptoms of diabetes can be controlled better when you are on a good exercise program. You will find that the body is able to metabolize the sugars that you are consuming much better when you are on this kind of program. Plus you are less likely to crave unhealthy and sugary foods so your insulin will not be under as much stress. If you are suffering from diabetes or pre-diabetes, it is best if you are able to get on a good workout program as soon as possible.

Mood

Your mood can be influenced by how much you exercise. Those who are depressed and down a lot of the time are the ones who rarely if ever get out there and do a good work out. Think about it this way, the few times that you have been to the gym and got in a really good workout how did you feel? Most people will say they felt good and that they were happy and on a little cloud for the rest of the day. Well, if you get on a good exercise program, you will be able to feel this way all of the time. Overall your mood will begin to improve. If you have depression, you may be able to cure it with a good exercise program. Even if you are not suffering from a mood disorder, you can benefit from the mood enhancement that comes from a good work out program.

Digestion

For many of those who are suffering from issues with their digestive tracts, a good work out program is able to help out with this. You should get in at least five days of moderate activity for 30 minutes on each day in order to see some of these great benefits on your digestive system in no time.

Self-confidence

For many, the way that they look and feel can determine how confident they are in themselves. When they start out on an exercise program and begin to lose weight, plus get all of the great health benefits that are listed above, they are going to feel a little bit better and you will notice a huge surge in the amount of self-confidence that they are feeling. They will begin to like the way that they look and will want to show it off. Just a few minutes of exercise each day can make this into a reality.

Conclusion

If you are trying to add more plants into your omnivorous or pescatarian diet or are trying to consider a more nutrient-dense palette of plants in a vegetarian or vegan diet, try to incorporate more whole foods and raw products, which have not been denatured due to heat and temperature. Here are some ways to start:

·   Blend more vegetables together into soups, stews, and curries or adding them with fruit for a healthy breakfast smoothie or snack.

·   Add 1-2 more vegetables into your sandwiches, stir-fries, and pasta dishes or make a garden salad as a side for your main meals.

·   Opt for fresh fruit with nut butter such as almond or peanut butter that provides the complete number of macronutrients as a snack on the go throughout the day as an energy boost.

·   Reach for a cold-pressed fruit and/or vegetable fruit juice with at least 3 different ingredients instead of a cup of java or caffeine

·   Add more vegetables to your breakfast first thing in the morning such as spinach, tomatoes, and mushrooms to an omelets or scramble will help you easily get more plants earlier on in the day.

It is important to note that high cooking temperatures and over-processing of many vegetables and fruit can denature and remove the health benefits of their nutrient profile. Once a week, try a raw diet where you incorporate at least one meal or juice with all raw vegetables and fruit. Spiralized salads, fresh vegetable sticks, fresh fruit salads, and cold-pressed juices can allow you to incorporate more fruit and vegetables without sacrificing textures, flavors, vitamins, and minerals. Be aware that not all vegetables can be consumed raw: those that contain starches such as potatoes, most squash varieties, sweet potato, and taro cannot be consumed raw as the gut cannot breakdown the heavy starches. Many leafy greens can be consumed raw such as spinach, kale, and arugula but others like swiss chard, mustard greens, and broccolini may taste less bitter if they were fried or boiled. Be aware that the volume of vegetables also decreases when boiled, so it may appear that you may need to consume more cooked veggies to feel fuller. Most legumes are highly undigestible without cooking them down. However, you can choose to sprout many legume seeds such as sunflower seeds, mung beans, radish seeds, and broccoli seeds. These can be used to garnish salads and soups with plenty of health benefits and anti-inflammatory properties. If you are ever craving animal products, seek out these healthy, plant-based alternatives:

- Nutritional yeast instead of parmesan cheese

- Coconut bacon instead of pork bacon

- Extra firm tofu instead of chicken breasts

- Roasted cauliflower instead of chicken wings

- Cashew sauce instead of cream cheese

- Coconut whip instead of whipped cream

- Portobello mushroom caps instead of beef steak

Nutritional yeast is nutty in texture but does not contain any dairy by-products. It is also not a traditional yeast product used in baking or in brewing beer as it is intended to be consumed as a food product. Look for fortified nutritional yeast whereby vitamins are added to the manufacturing process. One tablespoon of nutritional yeast contains all nine essential amino acids as a complete protein that is required for human consumption. It also contains many B vitamins and minerals such as selenium, zinc, and manganese. Nutritional yeast is very beneficial to gut health, fighting off inflammation in the intestines, and removing toxins from certain food products.

Coconut bacon does not contain any meat by-product but is a crunchy alternative to the heavily processed and fatty pork bacon. It is made by drying out pieces of coconut flesh. It still contains a high fiber and protein profile but also contains polyunsaturated and monosaturated fats that help to increase HDL good cholesterol, unlike pork bacon which contains lots of saturated fat and may enhance LDL bad cholesterol.

Extra-firm tofu can handle high cooking temperatures or can be consumed raw after fermentation. It can be crumbled or cut into steaks and offers a chewy texture with a high protein profile, comparable to chicken breasts. It is also neutral in flavor and can absorb moisture and different seasonings and liquids to enhance its taste profile.

Cauliflower has been used commonly to replace chicken wings on restaurant menus. The texture of cauliflower when roasted, is slightly nutty and very crunchy on the outsides, while the insides tend to be soft and chewy like chicken wings. Cauliflower has a very nutrient-dense profile with a large amount of protein, fiber, Vitamin C, and Vitamin K which is helpful in blood circulation and supporting the immune system. Because it is so neutral in flavor, it can take on many sauces, flavorings, and seasonings – you can use your favorite seasonings for chicken wings as you would for cauliflower!

Cashew sauce is surprisingly very creamy in consistency due to its high content in healthy fats. Using a ratio volume of 1:3, cashews to water, you can soak the cashews overnight and blend them together to create this versatile, dairy-free sauce without any additives or stabilizers! It can be used for both desserts and savory dishes and can be stored in the fridge for a few weeks. You can add anything from paprika, curry powder, cumin, turmeric, or chilli powder to flavor this sauce! Coconut whip is made from coconut milk, blended on high for a few minutes in order to allow the liquid consistency to thicken. You can choose to sweeten the coconut whip with maple syrup and nutmeg. It has a very creamy texture without sacrificing any of its health benefits such as providing Vitamin E and fiber. It can be added to fruit snacks and desserts, in place of artificial whipped cream that is high in trans-fat. Portobello Mushrooms are very flavorful with an earthy, umami profile, that is like meat without any animal by-products. It is dense with the ability to hold a lot of different flavorings, sauces, and seasonings that you add to it. You can bake it, stir fry it, or boil it in soups and it will add a rich texture. It has many different minerals such as selenium, copper, and B vitamins, providing many anti-inflammatory benefits.